BARRY BE

GOD, ME
AND THE
BLACKHORSE

Outskirts Press, Inc.
http://www.outskirtspress.com

Paperback ISBN: 978-1-4787-1880-2
Hardback ISBN: 978-1-4787-0480-5

TABLE OF CONTENTS

(L-R), Parry, Ron, Barry, Keith, and Gene line up in the dark in front of the Montgomery Blair House before shipping out to Fort Holabird.

CHAPTER 1

I started college in 1963, but I was too busy trying to grow up and avoid all the family problems that so many of us seem to have. My father worked for the church (read: not much money) and was usually working two or three jobs to support everyone. I was only sixteen years old when I started college not matured—I was left with no confidence or prior successes. I had no social skills, no money, no sports skills, as well as other problems.I had been too young, too small, and wildly too ignorant to know how to fit into a teenage society I just wasn't ready for focusing, much less understanding life plans. I went through four college majors by my senior year but hadn't focused enough on anything, and my grades were borderline. Alas, it was 1967 and the middle of the Vietnam war. I had studied theology for a while, but I didn't have good enough grades and wasn't certain that I would be a good minister. Failing a ministerial deferment, the only other option was to be drafted.

My best friend was one year behind me, and he had his problems: family, and so on. And he felt that he wasn't ready to go on and would have to be drafted as well. Two other friends of ours also decided to get drafted. So we arranged through our individual state Selective Service Boards to get us all to go in as one group at the college's local board. When I told my mother, she had an absolute fit. I wouldn't graduate. I would get hurt. I was insulting my father and mother, etc. It was a good thirty-minute tirade. But it had already been arranged, and there was nothing she could do about it other than harangue me. I was older than seventeen years old, and she couldn't touch me. My father never made a comment one way or another. He never told his kids what they had to do. He'd give you advice if you asked for it, and most of us kids did ask, but he didn't impose anything on anyone.

On the appointed day, we found three other college students also waiting. The seven of us boarded a bus to Fort Holabird (now gone) in Baltimore, Maryland. We went through the classic physical. We stood around in our skivvies in lines going through one station after another. We had the fun exam of standing in long rows in a large wooden room, all facing the front. We had to drop our shorts, bend all the way over, spread our butt cheeks, and maintain the position as the doctor with a large flashlight went down the rows examining our nether regions. There were a few trying to avoid the draft by pretending to be "strange" with their silk underwear, etc. They were not usually very successful. I broke a classic military rule by volunteering to type. It was only for the day, and it kept me busy. When everyone was done, we were sworn into the service, and we boarded another bus on our way to Fort Bragg, North Carolina.

At Fort Bragg, we began the process by the standard yelling of forming up, and we got marched to an empty wooden barracks, and the very basics were presented. It was very early, so we only got a few hours sleep, and we were yelled awake. We ran everywhere, and we began with running to chow. No talking, standing in line, and we were given a bowl, a glass and a spoon and out the door. We were sent to take tests. My score was high enough that they offered to have me go to officer candidate school, but I turned them down. We paraded through the clothes area where they guessed your size and gave you clothes. They weren't wrong too often, but some of it was unwearable. We got marched to the barbers. We had been warned that we had to bring money to pay the barbers who performed the sixty-second haircut. The rest of our group had gone first and were standing in a block formation waiting for us to finish. I came out and couldn't recognize my best friend to save my soul, and he was in the front line.

Later we were sent to medical for a brief exam, and we got our shots. At the time, the military used air guns to inject the shots into our arms. One tech was on each side as you wandered through in your shorts. It didn't hurt less than shots as you were using forced air to push the medicine in. Of course, if the medic didn't keep the gun dead flush against your skin, you could have a bloody mess. On our last day they took us out in a variety of trucks to load and carry. About 2:00 p.m. someone came yelling for me. "Where have you been?" They had lost me. I, of course, told them that I had been in that bay loading trucks. They couldn't harass me too much because our supervising sergeant was standing right there and our truck out hadn't moved. It happened that our plane flight to San Antonio was supposed to leave shortly, and they hadn't finished up giving shots, paperwork, eye test, etc. So they ran me through from station to station. "Where have you been?" at every stop. Then a couple arrogant Green Berets drove me in a hurry to the airport. They were quizzing me about where I was going, etc. When they found out that I was religious, the ribald questions began, and my complete inadequacies were reviewed at length. At last everything settled down, and we took off in a brightly painted Braniff Airways jet (now defunct) for the next step in the new adventure.

The first part of this book is about training and adapting to the military world. The second part is about my activities in Vietnam. I wrote the book a long time ago for my kids. I went to Nam with religious goals and standards that were far different than most. I still have them. But to maintain them, hard choices had to be made as to values and priorities. I hope that looking at my life may help you focus on the true values of your life's priorities.

I need to thank my wife, Sue, for helping me put this together and put up with me. I also need to thank John Cramer and Dale Shimel, fellow C Troopers, for their help.

This book is dedicated to the troopers of C Troop, 1st Squadron, the 11th Armored Cavalry Regiment of 1969 who fought, were wounded, or died for their country and for their comrades.

CHAPTER 2

Basic training would have to be the most deplorable single part of a military career, barring combat, that could occur. Every one of us has horror stories as to how tough it was, how evil the sergeants were, etc. Of course they took pride when they finished it. I was never in the Marines, so I'll let them win that argument about who's toughest. One has to admire their courage and esprit de corps. They take pride in their achievement, as they should. My whole idea of warfare was foreign to that mystique anyway. I was always uncertain that the best way to win a war, by being ugly, made any sense at all. The best way to win was to be smarter than your opponent, and if you would get them to be killed without ever risking your neck was a far superior way of warfare than to see how many times you could charge a machine gun nest and start a collection of Purple Hearts. Obviously, I didn't fit the idea of the best military material. But the book *The Art of War* certainly would back me up.

Basic training at Fort Sam Houston in San Antonio, Texas, was generally pretty easy. Our cadre were mostly lifers but some were specifically trained. Our DIs (drill instructors) wore their Smokey Bear hats and snarling dispositions, but in one sense we were an elite group. The majority of us were students at some level and were all highly motivated. We all had high moral standards, which meant that we were rarely rabble-rousers or misfits. Plus, a remarkably high number of us were college students at various levels. In my religion education was very strongly emphasized, and well over half of the students had some college education. Being a college student was not necessarily a blessing in basic training, but we were used to a rigid society where behavior that was "wrong" was not tolerated very much, and we had all grown up in a very conservative society where we didn't practice many "excuses" that others practiced. We were Christians who expected to accept authority, and rebellion was unusual. At least by many general standards. Hence, we weren't the threat to the DIs that many college graduates were even if we were smarter than the sergeants were. We were all together at Fort Sam because none of us would carry a weapon, which made us unique to start with. So, while we got our share of harassment, the cadre generally didn't hassle us too much. Partly, there wasn't all that much to hassle us about. I think that a great deal of it was they respected our ideals and performance.

After we arrived we had to wait around for over a week for basic to start as there weren't enough people there to fill a class. Mostly we just did clean-up and got a little used to the system. We had our own class cadre made up of people that the sergeants had selected to direct our class and keep general order. As these came from the earliest recruits to arrive there, the rest of us who arrived later just fit into the mob. There was one unexpected benefit from there being so many of us from the same religion. As none of us smoked, we discovered there were more non-smokers than smokers in the barracks. Relatively unusual for that era. This had one major benefit. The barracks had several butt cans. These were large painted tin cans filled with sand into which the cigarettes were to be placed. Adolescent smokers being what they were in general, the butts went anywhere they felt like throwing them. Out in the barracks that was a problem as the sergeants weren't very enthusiastic about a fire in the wooden barracks. Plus, the sergeants inspected these butt cans every day, and woe be it unto us if they were dirty. The non-smokers had an irritation building. It was not enough that we had to be out on the parade ground to duck walk, a kind of walk where you grabbed an ankle with each hand and then you walked across the ground, inspecting the grass in the cold and damp for more cigarette butts. But to have to clean up the barracks when we didn't even smoke seemed a tad too much. By a large margin we outvoted the smokers who then had to go outside to smoke with no butts in the inside cans. There were occasional minor victories.

With the onset of basic, we settled into a routine of getting up at 4:30 in the morning with reveille. This was followed by the morning ablutions, cleaning the barracks, etc. The beds had to be made so that a quarter would bounce off the blankets. Your foot locker had to be "just so," and perish the man whose alignment wasn't perfect. Your dress clothes, etc., that were on hangers, all had to face the correct way with buttons buttoned correctly, etc. All shoes had to be spit-polished. This is a process that took hours to accomplish the first time but which was an ongoing process to keep them that way. Usually you took some polish and water or spit or some other special concoction that you thought made it look better and then gleamed every part of the shoe. The idea was to cover every pore of the shoe leather until you had a perfectly smooth surface. It could easily take six hours to do a pair of shoes for the first time. Once you had it done, you had an immaculate shine that you could see your face in. Of course, if it was tarnished in any way, dusty, etc., you couldn't just buff it; it had to be re-perfected again. If you got too much polish on the shoe, then you could get cracks to show in the surface, and you have to remove it and then start over. Then you had to use polish or another product to polish the sides of the soles of the shoes. The laces had to be just the right length and in the right position. Once you finished your training, you might spring for a special Corfam shoe that always looked like they were spit-shined, but they were forbidden in training. You could also get gold-plated belt buckles to cut down the time you had to spend to make it look good. But we had to spit-shine our boots every day, as well as every other shiny article that we had. You could be inspected at any time, and you didn't dare risk the demerits.

This could be a real problem at times. Your clothes had to always be neat and perfect. You needed to keep a clean set of starched clothes at all times, and preferably two or three sets because you never knew when you might have to crawl through a ditch and then be inspected a couple of hours later. You learned to be sneaky and have extra belt buckles, pre-polished, waiting for an emergency. The starch in the clothes was heavily applied so that the legs and arms stuck together. You "broke starch" to put on a new set of clothes. It gave you great creases and looked neat but sure felt strange. The army did the laundry, but it took a few days, and things could always go haywire in a heartbeat. One had to always be careful.

The barracks were generally long two-story wooden buildings with a large open bay and a wooden floor. Downstairs there was a small room at one end for the sergeant and at the other end was the latrines (read: bathrooms). The latrines were open affairs with absolutely no privacy. For that matter, the bays were long, open, plain affairs with windows on each side, with equally no privacy. The bunks were double over-under cot-like beds with the ends on the center aisles and the other ends close to the windows. Each bed alternated between where the feet or the nose ended. The windows had to be opened at least four inches in the winter to ensure proper ventilation. This could be a real trial, and during the cold months and during the winter a variety of sneaky ways to close the windows were tried. It could get downright chilly at night in Texas.

Lights out was generally by nine o'clock, but GIs were often up later spit-shining their boots, sewing clothes, and so on. For a very severe inspection, guys might make their beds perfectly and then sleep on the floor so as to not mess the bed up, and then give them time to get other things done in the morning. There was, of course, a fire guard in each barracks plus those who were detailed to walk around the barracks at night.

At reveille everyone formed up in a square and then saluted the flag while a record played the music. Then we began cleaning up. This was followed by re-forming up for breakfast. We, of course, marched everywhere. This was followed by a strict set of rules as to how we could act. Every place you went had a different set of rules depending on how nasty people wanted to be. At the assembly center in North Carolina, before we made it to San Antonio, there were no glasses when you went to eat. You drank out of cereal bowls. You had four minutes from the time you entered the door until the time you walked out. There was no talking, as if there was any time to eat and talk when there was only four minutes. In basic, it wasn't usually that stiff, but it was close. You stood in line at parade rest, one pace apart, and moved up as the line moved. Parade rest is a position of semi-attention where the feet are split apart about eighteen inches and the hands are clasped behind your back. You can look around, but you can't talk. Usually you could choose what you wanted to eat, but you never got seconds, so you piled it up the first time. The food was generally pretty good, if a bit greasy and heavy on starches. You could have all of the milk that you wanted, but sodas and other goodies were not available. In basic, there was no chit-chatting in the mess hall (read cafeteria) but things lightened up later. Of course, one of the privileges of being in the army was the right of participating in the Kitchen Police. This euphemism for scut labor meant that you could be awaked at three o'clock in the morning so that you could peel potatoes, wash pots and pans, scrub floors, and perform other menial labor as assigned. Usually you got done at about seven in the evening. Of course, you were still expected to know what was taught to the others the days that you were at work. You also had to get the shoes polished, etc. for the next day.

During the day you were normally in classes of different sorts. You had classes on everything from military courtesy to using the radio. There were also several daily periods of PT (physical training) where the sergeants took turns trying to see how much they could make you look like fools. We had our own special masochist who was almost never there except for PT. He was a physical fitness buff who was delighted in making your body hurt while he harangued you about your inadequacies. Meanwhile, the other sergeants wandered about looking for the slackers and the weak, both of whom needed special attention.

Punishment for infractions took a variety of forms. Demanding that someone do extra push-ups was almost routine. It was particularly galling to have the class cadre harassing you. One of our class buck sergeants, while essentially a nice guy, had a tendency to harass some of the guys and give extra punishment. Over the weeks, he became particularly disliked so that one day, in an obstacle course, someone heaved a rock at him, that missed, but he decided that he really didn't need that position, and the sergeants gave me that position. It's amazing now, in one's ignorance, that you can take inordinate pride in things that in retrospect were so insignificant. I really felt good about the promotion, and it had its benefits and privileges all its own, but there wasn't any special promotions or ultimate changes in life. I once got yelled at on the obstacle course for being slow, and as a "sergeant" I was supposed to be the best. At least that was this lifer's opinion. I always was a mediocre physical specimen and wasn't very fast ever, least of all ever while I was on my back going under some barbed wire while someone was yelling at me. On the plus side, no one ever again made me do extra push-ups, so it wasn't a bad trade. I should explain the term "lifer" that I've already used loosely. The term "lifer," a derogatory term, referred to the term people used for those who made the army their career. They gave their life to the army, or any service, for that matter. As many of these were marginal candidates mentally, it was difficult to conceive of someone who enjoyed that kind of lifestyle, and we were rarely impressed by lifers.

Punishments came in several other styles as well. You could be out on KP, guard duty, or fire guard duty. You could physically harass them by putting them at attention, doing push-ups or other calisthenics, or simply destroying their beds as not being perfect. You could throw their spit-shined shoes out the window. They could keep everybody in formation or take away your weekend passes (a nasty punishment). If you really messed up, there was the Article Fifteen or even a court-martial. There are several different kinds of courts-martial, but I never heard of any being needed in our training ground. The Article Fifteen, however, wasn't all that rare. This was a summary punishment by the company commander that the GI agreed to. Theoretically, it didn't permanently go on your records, and you didn't run the risk of major punishment that a court-martial might mete out. You could be fined or have rank taken away. The other forms of harassment were certainly a problem with your life, but you wouldn't go to jail. Needless to say, no one ever wanted to run afoul of the C.O. (commanding officer). Actually, we rarely saw him as the unit was run by the sergeants and occasionally the lieutenant while the C.O. pushed papers in the office and ignored the scut work. You've all heard stories of GI's in a fight with a sergeant, but it never happened in my unit. They were forbidden to hit us, and we were pretty compliant anyway and nonviolent in addition. Surprisingly, we rarely got harassed in basic about being noncombatants. We only had basic for six weeks instead of eight weeks because there was no weapon training. We were offered that training but were not required to go to it. Again, we could attend a self-defense class but never had to use a rifle, pistol, grenade, or even a knife. The sergeants knew that except for occasional harassment of the weak, they could leave us alone.

Even the simple punishments didn't always work. We had one wiry guy from down on the farm who really got the sergeant unhappy. He was really a very nice guy who bothered no one but, like most of us, occasionally wasn't perfect. He had a belt buckle that had a smudge. One of the lifers said, "Give me twenty," meaning twenty push-ups. And you had to count each push-up. Faster than you could count, he had done the twenty push-ups. So the sergeant said, "OK, smart guy. Give me fifty." In less than two minutes, the fifty were done, whereupon he proceeded to do twenty one-handed push-ups with each hand, and he still wasn't breathing hard. The sergeant knew when he was licked and gave up, and he was never harassed again, and we all got great pleasure of the success of the little guy.

As training came to an end, we had some examinations, which were unforgettable. Our nighttime compass course was a mess. We were taken by a truck to some woods where we dismounted and divided into squads. We were given a compass and a compass course, and a flashlight was shined on the compass. This, theoretically, excited the phosphors so that we'd be able to read the compass in the dark. We were to walk a certain distance and then we'd come to a marker on the ground that had new directions. What a joke. We had only had one brief attempt before and never really got any training. Only two squads actually finished the course correctly. We also spent some time at Camp Bullis, an army camp about twenty miles north of San Antonio in the hill country. This was mostly sandy, open, hilly country covered with scrub brush and trees. We camped in the trees and got our first exposure to real weapons on the practice range. We had to crawl on our bellies under the barbed wire while machine guns rattled over our heads and small bombs went off around us. Of course, our crawling lanes never actually went under a machine gun, so unless you totally lost your mind and stood up and you crossed the firing lanes, you couldn't get hit, but it was stimulating to say the least. We also got some compass testing both in the day and at night while we were there. Here we had to cover large tracts of land using just a compass heading. Half a mile away there would be a series of stakes twenty feet apart, and we were supposed to, at the right stake, get another reading to some stakes, and so on. Most of us flunked this one. Reading a compass isn't all that hard, but practicing would have helped.

Most of us finished basic without any major problems or discipline. It helped to have a sense of humor so that you could laugh at the foolishness, but it wasn't that bad. They started to give us passes on Saturday so that we could go to church as basic training was over. This was a marvelous boost because our church operated a servicemen's center next to our church where we could relax, have a meal, and even sleep overnight on a bunk. We could meet other GIs (training on different week cycles) and associates in a Christian environment. It was a remarkable blessing to be able to step out after duty on Friday evening and go to the center. We could totally retreat and forget the army.

Generally, we had good memories with the irritation having long been forgotten. I can remember our head sergeant, Sergeant Moore, but I've forgotten everyone else. They were not hated, but I'm not in any hurry to go back again.

CHAPTER 3

AIT, or Advanced Individual Training, was the next big step to getting off of the bottom of the heap. I guess that I'm too much of a cynic, but the final ceremonies of basic training where families would come down and "celebrate" graduation always struck me as a little bizarre, as we were the lowest order of peons, and if you could chew gum and walk simultaneously, you made it through basic. But it is true that we would no longer be scum, having now graduated to scum first class. Actually, none of us were promoted by the army because you had to be in the service for eight weeks before you qualified to go to the next rank, the Private E2. An E2 was not really any rank, but it was a step up to private first class. And basic training without weapons training only gave us six weeks of training total. My good test scores qualified me for promotion, but I had to wait. This will be important later. At the moment, though, I wanted the few extra bucks that I would get paid, and it would speed up the next promotion. In point of reality, the extra rank would not give me any more authority or power. When I did get promoted, I would go from eighty-nine dollars per month to ninety-two dollars per month, plus it advanced you quicker, but I had to wait. The family of seven broke up here. We all had taken an aptitude test when we entered the service, and I knew that my scores were good, yet in the army's infinite wisdom, they sent the other six to Camp Bullis for driver training, and I went straight to AIT. The driver training was two weeks long, and this taught them to drive the big heavy army vehicles as well as maintain them. It also gave them a military driver's license. After completion, they went back to Fort Sam Houston to begin their medic AIT. It also put me two weeks ahead of my friends. We continued to see each other on weekends at church but only infrequently at Fort Sam.

AIT was held at the MTC (medical training center) at Fort Sam, about three-quarters of a mile away from where we had taken basic training. the barracks were the old wooden barracks, which was the standard for military bases since forever. And our routine remained the same. Only about ten of us went directly to AIT, and we were spread out in Charlie Company (C Company, to the uninitiated) so that we didn't have much interaction among each other. Things were a little stricter. We had our own sergeants supervising us. These were men who went to a special two-week school to teach them how to lead men. For most of us it was a laugh, but for some people, they would try anything to get ahead, even to listening to what the army told them. It was a mini-version of OCS (officer candidate school) where they got massive amounts of harassment to show that they were worthy. Sleep was at a premium in this kind of training, and they'd do pretty much anything, such as sleeping on the floor, to maintain their level of perfection. You didn't get much chance to correct any screwups, and many people washed out. All of those who became instant leaders got the privilege of leading us around for the ten weeks of AIT. I'm sure that it looked good on their records, and I guess that it might affect their getting promoted, perish the thought. You really did want to go to OCS, but my experience was that it was two weeks of guff in order to get ten weeks of guff. Because they were, of course, taught to command, as opposed to the enormously more difficult job of learning to teach, to say nothing of knowing how to lead. Most of them were misfits who were pretty much disliked and ignored whenever possible. You reap what you sow.

The next ten weeks were pretty much the same routine. Reveille was at 4:00 a.m. with formation, ablutions, breakfast, etc. in the same way. But there some new twists. The commander of the MTC was Colonel Charles Pixley. He was a physician whose proud boast was: "I am an officer first and a physician second," a minor contradiction of the Hippocratic Oath. He was a true lifer who meant to reach the top, and did. About ten years later, he became the surgeon general of the army. He used to drive around the compound standing up in the back of a specially modified jeep that had a bar across the back to hold on to. In this way, he would review the troops à la George Patton. What joy there was in our hearts as we waited for the ten seconds of glory as we stood at attention and he finally drove by. A couple of base MPs stopped him one day for driving around like that. MTC was only a small part of Fort Sam, and it was against regulations to stand up as you drove around. At any rate, within forty-eight hours, the two MPs had been transferred to Fort Hood up the road in Waco, Texas, the home of armor training. One really shouldn't mess around with full-bird colonels.

Another favorite stunt was the absence of wearing gloves while on parade. The gloves couldn't be used because none of the lifers wanted to take a chance on having the men look like sissies in the cold. So unless someone was particularly humane, you had to stand in the cold. No one wanted to be the first or only to allow the gloves to be worn. We froze our pinkies. Likewise, we couldn't use the drawstrings that pulled your jackets tight to keep the freezing air from going up and down your jacket. They made us remove the drawstrings so someone couldn't cheat and pull it tight. This would change the correct shape of the jacket and could be spotted easily that we were cheating. Besides, they needed to teach us humility. Waiting for the "man" was a cold chore.

Our classes were divvied up into three areas. There was first nursing science, where we taught everything from thermometers to making beds, to giving shots, to drawing blood, to starting IVs. The second area was the military sciences, which included carrying litters, making latrines, field hygiene, etc. We'd learn the commands to pick up a litter. Of course, because we didn't use it, except once on a test, we promptly forgot and ignored half of everything we were taught. For instance, not once in my career did I have four trained medics, or even two, who would be carrying a litter or certainly understood the commands. How about "Ready, lift" instead of "Litter post carry, move." And I'll guarantee you, if you were in a firefight, that no one stood up straight; we all couched over. Another part of pretty limited training was treating the sucking chest wound (described in another place). Assuming that we had every possible dressing, putting on dressings in combat was almost always when lying down, but they never taught us to improvise in real-life situations.

Classes were from about 8:00 a.m. to 12 noon and 1:00 to 5:00 p.m. If you missed classes because you were on KP, or sick call, or for any other reason, you were still responsible to know the material. There were no syllabi or textbooks to reference anything. Not that they gave you any study time, anyway. You got one test, at the end of ten weeks, out of the blue, and you had to know your material or you got a lower score, which could affect promotion. They had promised us that if you got a score higher than ninety out of one hundred, we could be promoted to PFC—equaled more pay/influence/etc. Some of the classes were a scream. Many of the classes were held in new classrooms, but most were still held in the old wooden buildings.

One class, in particular, stands out. It was held at 1:00 p.m. in an old building, and it was about one hundred degrees out. They had to close the windows and shades to show a movie about medicine in the military, this being an introduction about combat medicine in Korea. Having just eaten a lunch of spaghetti, the men were getting drowsy, and the movie droned on in the heat. About halfway through, it showed scenes of combat hospitals in surgery where you would see a surgeon deep in someone's abdomen. All at once he stood up, pulling out the guy's small intestines. He started running the small bowel through his hands, looking for shrapnel wounds. You can imagine the results. The guys would try to run outside, and a couple just didn't have time. The lifers thought that was a riot.

We were also theoretically taught how to read compasses and navigate in the dark, and the night they took us to the wooded field, shined a flashlight on a compass for about ten seconds, gave us a heading, and told us to follow the directions. Out of about twenty different groups, only one or two even finished, much less did it completely. None of us had the vaguest idea how to read a compass in the dark that didn't glow in the dark. And we had no other lights. We were supposed to find markers, but they were on the ground, and we could have stepped on them and wouldn't have known it. Perhaps this is a good time to review the old military word "snafu." This was originated in WWII and lightly translated as "situation normal all fouled up." During Korea, they felt that this wasn't complete enough, and they came up with "fubb," which stood for "fouled up beyond belief." And last, in Vietnam, they came up with "fubar." This stood for "fouled up beyond all recognition." Ours was only a "snafu," and we didn't enjoy getting harassed about our failure, of course, never having practiced it. I don't know what they expected. They probably changed our scores so that it looked good on the unit reports anyway.

Extra duties weren't too bad. We, of course, had fire guard duties in the barracks, but that rotated around sixty guys and wasn't much of a problem. Likewise, KP was infrequent, and the grief wasn't too much. Guard duty was equally a laugh. We'd walk around in the dark with a flashlight pretending things. I don't know who was protecting us, and there was the joy of presenting for duty, shined boots, "yes, sir; no, sir, general orders," etc., but generally it was a joke. Like everything else in the army, it was half serious and half a joke. We had a National Guardsman in one of our units who was a relief pitcher for the Cleveland Indians. Needless to say, duty for him was on a different scale than for us. A little showing off for the brass, of course, didn't hurt. Not that we weren't like him, but equality only existed in bunks and the minds of the inadequately trained.

After the third week of training, we were allowed a pass on the weekends. For the SDAs, this was a gift as we went to the center and stayed there Friday night, ate decent food, got a good Sabbath rest, etc. We showed up on Sunday morning in exchange for the others showing up Saturday, but usually there were no duties to speak of. I did get harassed for a couple weeks. One of our SDAs won the pool tournament at the USO club on Friday night. With good reason, the other GIs wondered why he could get off when they couldn't as he obviously (and by extension all SDAs) only preached a good line but did whatever they wanted. What they forgot was that when you got drafted, they asked what your religious preference was, not did you attend or even care about your religion. Having been raised an SDA, he said he was an SDA. He just never came to church but did whatever he wanted. Things eventually blew over, but things were sticky for a while. Sometimes I present a cynical picture of the army, and I sometimes paint it all black. We knew there was a war on and many of us would go to Vietnam. There was always a low-grade anxiety about that, which the army used, of course. They would guarantee us a cushy post if only we'd enlist for two mores years and go to such and such a school for training. But we could still take pride in ourselves. There was a certain patriotic warmth in a mass parade with everyone stepping tall and looking good. There was pride in our unit and ourselves, although never in our officers and rarely in our sergeants. We had a gung-ho short second lieutenant who was a lifer's dream. He'd bark orders in the best style, inspect, and harass us, give out petty discipline, etc. We did have a good drill sergeant, complete with Smokey Bear hat, who harassed us some but not much. He was more concerned with us and how we did. You always dislike sergeants, but we respected in turn and would easily have followed him. The third Louie was an unmitigated pain in the butt who would easily have qualified as a candidate for getting fragged in Nam. You can be a martinet and get away with it if you have good skills or you're good. He was neither. By this point, we had accepted harassment and nonsense duties as part of life. But most of us were experienced and intelligent enough to recognize competence and incompetence.

There were a few poor souls, however. We had a guy who at best qualified for a warm body in the scale of GI humanity. He was nice enough; he just wasn't working with a full deck in the IQ department. He sent his laundry in, but it got sent in without his name, or got lost, or he didn't pick it up, or whatever. At any rate, he began to get that special aroma of the unwashed. He'd get hints and suggestions, but it got worse and worse. Finally, he couldn't be ignored, and the sergeants discovered his ineptitude. He was thrown in the shower fully clothed and washed that way, under supervision; then he dressed in his dress uniform until his other clothes came back. One of our fellow medics was in the category of "screwup." Way back in basic, he ran into a tree and lost his teeth. Eighteen months later, we were in the same regiment in Nam, and I met him there. He still didn't have any teeth.

The food was basically edible if not cordon bleu. It was heavy on basics, and grease; it was nonetheless filling. Mealtimes were always looked forward to because there was unrestricted talking and a little extra time for monkeying around while people were eating. Every now and then we'd throw in a few rounds of the current risqué, derogatory songs while in the mess hall. That was great fun as the sergeants would run around screaming at us to be quiet and generally insulting us. One would look our way, and we'd shut up while everyone behind him would keep singing. We never pushed our games too far, though. Nobody wanted KP or guard duty, and the mess hall sergeants basically were decent guys who left us alone as much as possible.

About six weeks into the ten-week course, two events occurred of some significance. First, there was a competition for being the best student in AIT. To encourage us, they promised a promotion to PFC (or E3 pay grade) to everyone who got over nine hundred out of a possible thousand points. I was better than that, so they had an exam among the candidates in the company. I came in second because I couldn't remember the name of the carotid pulse, having been on KP that day. The winner of our company went on and took the trophy. I eventually graduated with a final score of 945, but I didn't get promoted. More about that later.

The second significant thing was that I ran into John K., a buddy of mine from college. He and I had sung in a sixteen-voice music group, called Pro Musica, that specialized in religious and renaissance music. I was the last of the sixteen to be picked, but John K. had a good voice. He had been drafted ahead of us and while at basic had formed a quartet with some other SDAs and sang together. It so happened that we had an SDA chaplain on the base who arranged the quartet and created it as a good morale and evangelism booster. The first guy in the quartet to make it through AIT got into personnel (I think with a few strings pulled), who then arranged to get orders out for the next three to get to keep the next three at Fort Sam. John K. couldn't and wouldn't pull any strings for me, but he did tell me how and where to go to be interviewed for a teaching position period. The army needed teachers, and most of the teachers were medics and NCOs. As a near graduate of college, I certainly qualified as smart enough, and I had the thought that perhaps I would qualify for the position. So, an appointment was set up for me to go over and meet a lieutenant colonel (a lady nurse) in charge of nursing sciences, an appointment that astounded my company cadre, who wondered how I got to meet these people. And sure enough, when orders came out, I was assigned to nursing science as an instructor.

This all came about the tenth week of AIT, and as most of my company got sent to Nam, it seemed the bright thing to do at the time. Many of the members of my church worked it out to get drafted in time to get assigned to Operation White Coat, a program held at Fort Detrick, in Frederick, Maryland, where they were assigned as medics. In exchange for this program, they became guinea pigs for medical research where they had research into various diseases. They agreed to be inoculated twice a year and could be infected or could be a double-blind patient for the research. The had their two-year stint there in Maryland and didn't have to go overseas. To the best of my knowledge, no one had ever died or even suffered permanent harm. Most of us would have jumped at the chance to spend our two years in Maryland in exchange for going to Nam. The only way to get into the program, however, was to have AIT or basic when the recruiting team came to Fort Sam to visit. I had missed them, so teaching had seemed to be a good deal.

We had a break partway through AIT for the Christmas holidays, and we got to fly back home, and it was certainly exciting. I know my family never saw a pair of shoes that looked that good from my hands before. The highlight of the season was a Party where my now-wife and I announced our engagement. Needless to say, our vacation was too short. It was certainly strange to be wandering around in uniform with a bald head. There was an odd mixture of pride in the uniform, chagrin at my total lack of any ribbons, rank, etc. We didn't even have a sharpshooter's badge as we hadn't trained with weapons. Likewise, there was a curious mixture of bravery for being in the service, becoming a man, defending your country, etc. versus the baby-killer status that some imputed to all soldiers. It was a funny emotional era.

As AIT came to a close, we were getting excited about finishing, partly as to where we were all going, special training, etc., and partly because some would be protected. You had to be in the service for sixteen weeks in order to make PFC, and I would qualify by the end of my training period. The boy who beat me in the company competition won the training center competition. He and everyone else got promoted. I did not. I had a score of 945, with 900 being necessary for promotion. But I got overlooked. Because I didn't know about it until the last days of training but there was nothing I could do about it, and I became a Private E2.

CHAPTER 4

As a new instructor, I was officially ordered to become a member of the Headquarters Company of the MEDICAL TRAINING CENTER. They had nice new barracks and a considerably more laid-back approach to life. Formations and inspections were few and far between. At the absolute most, they were weekly, and even then they were cursory. Our hair had to be cut, but we didn't have to be skinheads. Beds had to be made, and clothing had to be picked up, but you didn't have to bounce quarters off of your beds or eat off of the floor. There was no KP (hooray!) or other general scut work. I could only remember personally speaking to my commanding office once during my whole tour there.

Before beginning teaching, I had several other classes first. I began with two weeks of nursing on the gastroenterology ward at Brook Army Medical Center. This was an imposing building at the end of the imposing parade ground at Fort Sam Houston. It was the army's main burn ward and was the center for many of the serious wound care problems for the patients from Nam. I can still vividly remember getting on an elevator to go upstairs, and I was followed by a gurney with a burn patient that had just been transferred from a plane from Nam. The burn ward was very large, and the odor was hard to adjust to. I was working hard to not vomit on the elevator. Military hospitals had their own special set of rules. Everyone had to get up and make their own beds at 6:00 a.m., and they didn't get back to bed until that evening unless they had a specific order from the doctor. They went to get their medicine from the nurse and not vice versa. On the one hand, I didn't learn too much when I was there; they didn't expect much as I had only a few skills, and I didn't stay long enough to accomplish much. On the other hand, it did give us exposure to the hospital and the military system.

This was followed by a one-week course in audiovisual aids. It had never dawned on me that someone needed a course on how to use a slide projector or a movie projector, to say nothing about using a cassette player. But considering some of the people we had in the service, it was probably a good idea. I learned next to nothing, but I did get a certificate showing that I was now certified to be able to run a cassette player. This is an honor that to this day brings oohs and ahs. I also took a two-week course on instructing GIs. You can imagine that one didn't earn too many skills in a two-week block of instruction, but then, you didn't have to have too many skills to be an instructor. Like many comments about the military, that's both true and false. The army wanted college graduates, educated people, to be your teachers. They obviously wanted people of intelligence and character. They wanted people who would be responsible and who could speak well and clearly. They wanted people who could communicate eloquently and who could be complete in what they presented. What they didn't need were orators and creative thinkers. In the army, the lesson plans had already been made up to meet some poo-bah's standards. Whether they were right or wrong, they were based on the military's many needs. To be fair to them, it wasn't always apparent to us new people, of course, who knew more than they did. We were asked to practice lesson plans from cover to cover. Nothing could be left out. If some one word was omitted, then one was reviewed with fear and trepidation. Presenting your lecture in a monotone voice was not recommended, but no great deal of time was spent working on you either. In its strictest sense, we were presenters, not teachers. If the course was a lecture, then we did a lecture. If there was some extra time to the course, then some teaching might be possible in an interpersonal way. As a peon who wasn't either a nurse or an officer, I'm certain that it never entered anyone's mind to consider using his or any other draftees as consultants for lesson plans or teaching techniques. Four years of college and training provided no qualifications other than preparing for war.

I then socially joined the nursing sciences branch of the Medical Training Center. Life settled down into a relatively non-stressed, structured lifestyle. There was little hassle, but there was direct responsibility. At the beginning, you were just an assistant. Someone with more responsibility, rank, or experience would be in control of the lecture. You waited until the class broke up into sections for individual training. For instance, you might follow them on one-on-one for injections, temperatures, putting on sterile gloves, etc. Of course, we were supposed to be observing how the sergeants taught as well. The students only had one chance to practice something, and my job would be to make certain that everyone knew that one item that day.

There was a variety of classes that one had to pass. Teaching hospital bed making was nothing special. Taking rectal temperatures was a gem. While no one liked to do it, and you had to do it on the other classmates, the black recruits wanting nothing to do with looking at someone's butt much less spreading the cheeks and putting in a thermometer. I can't say that I blamed them. The injection class was also fun. You started with your lecture and split into groups. You began with the morphine syrette, which had a very short needle and a metallic foil, soft, squeezable body that you just jammed into the body and squeezed. You could get some big galoot from the farm who could castrate hogs, stick the syrette in, and he'd pass out. To the delight of everyone. Using real syringes (made of glass back then), you had to teach the art of shoving it anywhere. For practice, we used the arms. If you had bad luck, you could get as a partner one of the "afraid" medics who would bounce the needle off the skin and have to try again, to the chagrin of the "patient." Worse was the aggressive medic who thrust the syringe into the bone so hard that the syringe would be bouncing up and down, stuck in the bone, while the patient was getting light-headed. The girl medics weren't any better. The class on starting IVs was sticking a syringe into a rubber tube in a fake arm. Also a lot of fun.

Military discipline in the classroom was controlled by the cadre. Just as the teacher *had* to read the lesson plan word for word, the student *had* to pay attention. Obviously, one couldn't guarantee that people would pay attention, but the students definitely couldn't fall asleep. If one felt sleepy, they were to go to the back of the room and stand up at attention. The class cadre had the responsibility to be certain that everyone was paying attention. Consequently, especially on warm Texas summer days, the cadre would be walking up and down the aisle making certain that everyone was awake. At the start of class, they were marched in to the classroom and stood at attention until the class commander reported to the instructor. At their command, they would be seated, and all the room was filled in from the front in order to hear my dulcet prose. If someone was drowsy, the cadre would nudge them or have them stand at the back. If they were drowsy in back, they were made to stand at attention in the back. If that didn't work, they were put in the front leaning rest position. This was an army euphemism for the push-up position, which becomes very uncomfortable remarkably quickly. Believe it or not, I once observed a class where one poor slob was actually asleep in the front leaning rest position. He had locked his arms and his back was sagging, but he was still officially in position and definitely asleep. The worst one was the dying cockroach position on your back with both arms and legs in the air. Generally the lower-grade instructors, the college draftees, were pretty laid back and didn't hassle the classes much. The lifer sergeants were a mix, however. Most were good to be around, but some were definitely in the pain in the gluteus maximus category. If too many people were sleeping, they might put the whole class at attention. They might chew out the cadre if they were really put out, or they might even call the company later to report their behavior, a not very nice thing to do. Needless to say, most thinking people tried to liven the class a little. Usually you tried a few jokes at the beginning, and usually another one in the middle of the lecture. As was to be expected, most of the jokes were less than pristine, pure. I had trouble in that area because I just didn't want to start a collection of off-color jokes. For a while, I tried using puns, but so many people just don't understand puns. I never came up with a really satisfactory answer to good humor for GIs. There were some WACs stationed at the MTC also going through medic training. It was always fun teaching them, if only because they were so different from the GIs, especially to look at. They could be as crude as the male GIs, if not some different, but just as filthy. The WAC soldiers were about as ugly as you could have possibly believed. Granted, neither males nor females looked wildly attractive with shaved hair and hairdos. The uniforms weren't terribly attractive as well. The male GIs complained regularly of how ugly the female GIs were. Obviously both genders had attractive GIs. My opinion, after some observation, was that neither gender had any good reason to complain about the other.

The Nursing Science branch was run by nurses, all officers, of course. The commander was a lieutenant colonel who was also a very nice lady as well as being a nice person to be around. She was an artistic person as well. The assistant commander was a dumpy female major who was the opposite of the colonel. She was true "lifer" material without the slightest trace of a sense of humor. Fortunately, I didn't get to know Major Sullivan well, and the one time I did was not pretty. The branch was divided into three parts, each commanded by a captain or a lieutenant, either male or female. Again, all nurses. The nurses taught the advanced lectures only. These could be IV therapy, medications, and so on. They left the mundane lectures to the peons. The one time that I had a "close" meeting with Major Sullivan happened because of a class to teach the GIs how to put on sterile gloves. As you can imagine, it would have been very expensive to really have sterile gloves, so they would wash and powder the old gloves, some of them very old, to be used in the exercise part of the class. In this class, I had a sergeant first class assisting me (read, supervising my skills). The first half of the class was lecture. In the second half, we would show them how to take the gloves out of the wrap sterilely and put them on properly. I made a big boo-boo. I told the class to be careful not to pull too vigorously on the gloves because some of them were too old (you could see the cracked rubber) and we didn't want to tear the gloves. The E-7 sergeant, rather than make a comment to me about not saying that, or have the captain talk to me, went to Major Sullivan. She proceeded to call me on the carpet at attention. I was denigrating the army. Think of all the men dying in Vietnam and their sacrifices, and here I was saying these awful things, etc., etc. I had better get my act together. She'd be watching me. I was the lowest kind of person. I was so frustrated that I was in tears, if only because I wasn't allowed to say a thing, and I was being abusive and evil. Over cracked rubber, as well. She never gave me an opportunity to reply. This probably convinced her how bad a person I was, and I'm certain that she put me on the list for Nam. I can guarantee you that I was very careful around the lifers.

I had one other encounter with officers during my stay there. About two months into my stay, it became apparent that I wouldn't get my promotion. My commander wanted us to all have rank, if only so that we could have prestige over the recruits as opposed to being a rankless nothing. She arranged to have me see the commanding officer of C Company because only he could authorize it. Upon presenting myself for my appointment, I got ushered into his office where he, his sergeant, and his assistant were all waiting. Because this appointment was made at the request of the colonel, he had to grant it, but he wasn't going to let her tell him what to do. It was all very formal and rigid and, of course, I got nowhere. I didn't even get an explanation. So much for my score greater than ninety and coming in second in the contest. I still hadn't learned to work the military system. As for much of life, being in the right has no bearing with reality. It's how much pressure you can apply. I had none and got treated like it. It was two months before I could be promoted. It sounds like sour grapes, but that promotion totally changed my whole life. I started at MTC in April and got orders for Vietnam in October. I would take leave in December and then report to Vietnam after Christmas, when I only had nine months left to serve. If I had had my promotion, I wouldn't have gone because they didn't send specialists fifth class to Nam on a first tour, only the fourth-class specialists.

The fall before I got my orders, I played football for the MTC. Our church didn't like aggressive sports, so I had limited skills in football or any contact sports. I had only played tag or flag football but never tackle football. In the army, of course, it was only tackle football, and me with my no violence background. Being semi-clumsy and certainly untrained, I got stuck on the second-string line, as could be expected. I didn't enjoy getting hurt and hadn't learned to "kill" the other person in spite of what your body was doing. The other reason was that I wasn't a loudmouth, glad-hander, officer, or star, and that was the only way to get a skill position. We had a very good quarterback who was also a teacher and who could also have played semipro ball right then. I well remember the first time we put on pads. I had trouble putting on a lineman's cage, much less knowing how to play lineman. Our offensive center was a short five-feet-seven-inch gung-ho player with lots of experience. He was a nice guy, until he put the pads on. On the first play from scrimmage, he did a forearm shiver and put his fist between the cage and my nose. You know how you can see stars in the comics? Well, I literally could see nothing but stars and felt nothing but pain. The very next play, he did it again. I'm glad he was on my side because who knows how he treated the opponents. We had a good season and won one of the two trophies. We came in second that year, which wasn't bad, considering the transient nature of the staff. Colonel Pixley was all proud of his boys and invited us down to his headquarters and gave us a trophy and had our picture taken. In retrospect, it was fun even if I was a klutz.

About June of that year, I applied for leave and discovered that I had to have permission from the army to get married. Fortunately, my commanding officer didn't give me any flak about it, but could have. It never dawned on me that I needed his permission. My bride had done all the work as I was obviously not available. We didn't have much money with me being in college and being in the army, so it wasn't a very fancy wedding. I was the last one to know when I was going to be able to leave and got there two days before the wedding. My father gave the service, and we had a small reception before taking off in a used Rambler towing a small trailer with our worldly goods. We stopped at a motel in southern Virginia for the night, and we were going to go to Gatlinburg in the Smokies the following day, but like most things in my life, the plans never came off. The poor Rambler's transmission gave out in Knoxville, and we had to get it fixed. We spent two days in a dumpy motel doing nothing waiting to get the car fixed and afraid to spend any money because we didn't have much. And we didn't know how much it was going to be. Three hundred dollars later we took off again (this was 1968 money, mind you). We got as far as Waco, Texas, before it gave out again, with our new transmission. My leave time was up, and I had to get an extension for two days (bless their hearts, they believed me), which gave us time to take the bus to San Antonio so that I could report. Some people would consider me a goody-goody, but at this stage I think that I was really just trying to do things the way that I thought a Christian should. And every now and then, alas, not with any verifiable consistency, this attitude paid off because they wouldn't hassle me. They knew that I wasn't a rabble-rouser or an abuser of the system. Later, a friend who had a car drove me back up to Waco to pick up the newly repaired buggy.

We settled into an apartment about two blocks from the church but only stayed a short while before we moved to another nicer place closer to the church. My wife got a job as a secretary on the west side of San Antonio, and this was the first in a long line of superior jobs for her employers. In all of the years that she worked for different employers, there has never been one who hasn't wanted her to stay on. They've all loved her. Me, they haven't been so sure about, but everyone loved her. By then, I was a specialist fourth class, and the extra money helped out some. In October, my orders for Nam arrived, so we had to make new plans.

In November, we had Vietnam training that everyone going to Nam had to take. This was a one-week course that was to prepare us for warfare in Nam. Most of it was typical garbage. For instance, we had a lecture on message coding but never got a chance to use it or practice it. Of course, I promptly forgot it. Nine months later when I conceivably thought that there might be a time that I needed to use it, I couldn't remember it. We had a sergeant who was telling us about his unit in Nam that had carved a large base camp out of the jungle and the attacks and trials that they had endured. There was a large mountain overlooking the camp, and sappers had crawled underneath the wire and overrun the camp. I couldn't remember the name of the unit, but two months later when I arrived by airplane at the camp, I remembered the camp. They took us down a booby-trapped trail and demonstrated the different kinds of ways that you could get mutilated in the jungle. It was all very reassuring. I doubt that we learned anything of value, but it certainly did raise our anxiety levels.

Unfortunately, by about six months of married life, we were back at home where we had started, and I had to leave for the Far East. I got a thirty-day leave before I had to report, and we drove back, the first of many moves. We moved into the basement of my father's house, and she got a job. We had a limited holiday season, but we did have Christmas. I had worked in a local department store to earn some money for the holiday, but I had to fly to San Francisco four days after Christmas to begin the next great adventure.

CHAPTER 5

I arrived in San Francisco the evening of the 28th of December and got a room in the YMCA to save money as I didn't have to report until the 29th. The following morning, I took a bus across the Oakland–San Francisco Bay Bridge to the Oakland Army Depot and signed in. As with all such places, you quickly became just a number that they pushed along. They didn't hassle you too much, if only because they had enough to do. There was an enormous polyglot of personalities, the vast majority of whom were draftees and first-time warriors who spent their time almost exclusively wondering what was going to happen. The various personalities were fabulously interesting. The macho boys all wanted to be in a combat unit where they were going to get medals and kill a lot of gooks. The worriers were generally quiet and stewed a lot with the hysterical fringe unable to keep quiet at all.

All such bases are huge rumor mills. Everyone's being assigned here or there, or we're all going to get this duty, etc. The lifers, all of whom had more rank than the lowly draftees, all knew where they were going and generally didn't spend any time with us, if only because they had different quarters, mess halls, and so forth. The next day, being Friday, I was wondering about going to church, duties, and so forth. Bless their hearts, the army said that I could leave as long as I reported back in time. I called the local church, and as the good Lord willed, the pastor was there to take the call. He arranged to pick me up and took me to church. I had dinner afterward and had a really good time. It showed me that growing up in the church and my father being in education had a real value. Having made relationships made a difference. The pastor didn't know me or know my father, but he knew about my father, which didn't hurt. Sadly, I lost his name and address and wasn't able to send him a letter. The visit was very refreshing and a fine counterpoint to the anxieties of going to Nam.

We finally boarded a plane at a local air force base and began the first phase at about 11:00 p.m. This was a stretch DC8 leased from a commercial carrier that had 215 seats and 215 bodies and no first class. There were three stewardesses who, while they weren't ugly, weren't in danger of being assaulted by the GIs either. Most of us were moderately tired but got only fitful sleep, being crammed into the seats and filled with wonder. We arrived in Honolulu at 3:00 a.m., which meant, of course, that none of us saw anything of the islands. We wandered through the airport with all of the shops closed and then re-boarded after they had gassed up for the next leg. This was a twelve-hour stretch to Clark Air Force Base in the Philippines and was one of my more forgettable plane trips. Meals consisted of box lunches with warm milk, two pieces of bread with some indescribable meat without mayo or condiments, etc. Likewise, there were no movies, magazines, blankets, or other amenities. At Clark, we couldn't go anywhere either, and it was a military base, so we couldn't scram anywhere if we had wanted to. The last leg was a short hop across the China Sea to Nam. In this case, we went to the Bien Hua Air Base in southern South Vietnam. It was hot and sweltering, of course, and we were wearing US Army fatigues, which didn't help any. They'd taken away much of our clothing in San Francisco, and we were given jungle clothing shortly after arrival. From Bien Hua, we were bussed through some villages, many having obviously been bombed or been in the middle of firefights, to the 90th Replacement Battalion at Long Binh, our next home.

The country of South Vietnam was divided, for military purposes, into four corps, with the First Corps, or I Corps, in the absolute north next to the demilitarized zone (DMZ). The Fourth Corps, or

IV Corps, was in the absolute south of the country and included the flat Mekong Delta region full of swampy land and rice paddies. The country runs roughly north and south with a spine of rugged jungle mountains running north and south along the western edge of the country. As far as moving troops in and out of the country, there were two large bases. Cam Ranh Bay was in the north-middle of the country on the coast, and Long Binh was the large base camp in the south. As Saigon was in III Corps, Long Binh handled this area. Long Binh was a huge base camp of almost eighty-nine square miles. It had a skeet range, miniature golf course, theaters, swimming pools, multiple PXs, etc. Bien Hua was a huge air base about a dozen miles away. Plus, Tan Son Nhut Airport was twenty miles away in Saigon. The 90th was a small block of Long Binh, and we arrived on the 31st without the vaguest idea of what was happening. Basically, we had no duties except to show up twice a day for roll call when orders were posted. Alas, likewise, we couldn't go anywhere or do anything either. That night, we were soundly asleep in our bunks when people started firing on the perimeter, not too far away. The response was a riot. Most were confused and a little anxious. Some just grabbed their mattresses and rolled off their top bunks onto the floor, *kla-bam*, as if their mattresses were going to provide much protection. It took a few minutes to figure out that it was New Year's and the guys on guard were just having a little fun. Mostly we just wandered around, looking at name lists and wondering where we would go, when would we go, was it a hospital or combat, and so on.

Two days after arriving orders came for about a dozen of us to go to the 11th Armored Cavalry Regiment at a place called Xuan Loc. Not a one of us had the foggiest idea who or what that was; neither did we know where it was. Nobody else seemed to know either. At the right time, they put us in a bus and took us back to Bien Hua and dumped us at a small building with an open space covered with a tin roof where we sat and waited, still knowing nothing. After an hour, we were sent to a puddle-jumper airplane called a Caribou, and away we went. This was an interesting airplane that for obvious reasons did not follow FAA regulations very closely. The seats were just thin nylon that hung between aluminum struts that ran up through the middle of your crotch. Every air pocket gave new meaning to the words "scrotal support." After a couple of stops, the pilots, in order to gain altitude as quickly as possible, stood the plane on its wing at the end of the airstrips and climbed back up the other way, demonstrating that the flying was probably safe but was distinctly exciting to the uninitiated.

We were dumped at one end of our base camp in the middle of nowhere. While sitting in the middle of the short airstrip, we passed around news of the US, families and girlfriends, anxieties, etc. One of our guys gave us a long spiel about his various previous duties as a medic in Nam, but we were a little skeptical. And as often was the case with the humanity that we met, we later discovered that he hadn't been in Nam before at all; he was just feeding us a line to earn some respect. Needless to say, he ended up losing what little we had of him in the first place. We found out later that we were at a base camp called Blackhorse about forty miles east of Saigon and about six miles south of a small town called Xuan Loc (Swan Lock).

After over an hour, someone came and picked us up and took us to the headquarters troop of the 11th Cavalry. The 11th Armored Cavalry Regiment (ACR) was the first armored unit to be in Vietnam. It was sent there as a trial to see if armor could work in Vietnam with its jungles and mountains, and it remained the only independent armored unit in the country, everyone else being a part of a particular division. As an independent, we were assigned particular tasks to different divisions as some creative mind thought them up. As a gung-ho unit, we had General Patton's son George as our commander at that time when I was there, and the leaders were out to prove how good and tough we were. And we went everywhere. To the best of my knowledge, we were the only unit to work in the jungle as well as just run the roads and the flat rice paddies.

The Cav was an interesting unit divided into three squadrons plus support facilities, such as the medical unit to which I was officially assigned. In reality, the medical unit was only supportive and in particular only worked for the base camp staffing because any real casualties were med evac'd to the nearest trauma hospital. Each squadron consisted of three troops and one tank company. The tank company consisted of three platoons of three M48 fifty-two-ton tanks each, plus their support personnel: cooks, administration, repair facilities, and huge tank retrievers to bring them in, etc. The three troops consisted of three platoons plus a headquarters unit. The combat platoons originally consisted of what we called ACAVs, or armored cavalry assault vehicles. These were boxy thirteen-ton aluminum-alloy-armored personnel carriers that were modified to carry a thirty-caliber M60 machine gun on each side, with a slanted gun shield for each, plus a fifty-caliber machine gun in front in the middle of a round metal cupola in which sat the commander of the vehicle. There was also a driver who sat up front on the left. He had a seat that he could drop down in combat, and he could look through periscopes, but usually he drove with his seat up as he could see better and get a breeze as well as get partially away from the engine. The front, over the engine, was slanted back to make bullets bounce off it. The back end could fold down for loading. The top rear end of the vehicle had a large square hatch that would open up over the back. The ACAVs had tracks on each side like a caterpillar and could, with some limitations, go anywhere. Besides the basic weapons and the crew of four, each vehicle carried 15,000 rounds of thirty-caliber ammo and 7,500 rounds of fifty-caliber ammo; plus, each man had an M16 with 2,000 rounds of ammo, an M79 grenade launcher with two hundred rounds, and assorted other paraphernalia such as flares, grenades, claymore mines, etc.

The headquarters platoon consisted of the captain's vehicle, a medic track that was kept mostly empty to have room for carrying wounded on stretchers, a mortar track that had a 4.2-inch mortar inside, plus, of course, the support personnel of administration, cooks, etc. Just when I arrived, although I didn't know it at the time, we had just been issued the Sheridan tank, a seventeen-ton aluminum tank with a 152 mm cannon on it. This was neither as strong nor as powerful as the M48 tanks in the tank company, but it did have a bigger cannon. Each combat platoon replaced three ACAVs with three Sheridans, which left each platoon with three tanks and six ACAVs. That's a lot of firepower, and whatever happened to the Cav in combat, we were never in the position where we got overrun because we ran out of ammo.

As a medic, I was assigned to the medical company for the regiment and began with just the very simplest of duties, including KP, etc. Again, we had absolutely no idea of what to expect or look for. Almost no one told us anything or any of the options that we might have. We, of course, continued to speculate on where we'd go, etc. Some were anxious to get into a combat unit, others didn't want to, and some were fatalistic. I didn't know enough to know what was best. I had certainly learned that in the army you got sent to where they wanted and you did what they said. Usually you got no options at all. One thing was certain: in a combat unit, there was bound to be less scut work than rear camp garbage. We had one little loudmouth kid who knew he was going to be a hero and told us so. Thus, about two weeks after I arrived, they were looking for a couple of volunteers to go to one each of the combat troops, and he and I took it. As the newbies without any special skills, we were going to go sometime, and getting it over with was better than sitting and waiting. I gathered my gear while the other guy ran over to report. Because he had first choice due to his speedy run, he chose the howitzer battery as they were going out right away. This was a unit that consisted of self-propelled 155 mm howitzers. The irony being that they generally weren't shot at at all; rather, they were farther back and fired artillery fire to the forward units who needed help. Whereas I, by my "sloth," arrived in time to be assigned to C Troop, one of the combat troops who were in camp for four weeks to learn how to use their newly assigned Sheridan tanks. Of some interest, about four months later, our hero shot himself in the foot, ostensibly while cleaning his pistol, in order to get out of Nam.

Officially, I was assigned to the Headquarters Troop of the First Squadron, which contained a medical unit with a physician, Doctor Cupps, a DO from the Midwest, an LPN, several medics, and an officer who specialized in medical unit administration. The doctor, a captain, was a first-class guy. Besides knowing what he was doing, he considered you a human being and not a war body because you didn't wear bars on your shoulders. I stayed with the HHT (Headquarters and Headquarters Troop) for about two months and got broken in to the basics of being a rear base medic. We still had KP and other scut, but usually it was pretty laid back. There was sick call every day, but sick patients weren't very common. I learned how to play solitaire during long, boring evenings and nights in the clinic. There were a few interesting incidents. I was assigned to a small jeep with a stretcher, which I was to take care of. They gave me a military driver's license (which my basic buddies took a two-week course for) just by me giving them my name because they needed a driver. Xuan Loc was mostly off limits, but I got down there once to pick up someone. I never got into any of the buildings, the local clubs with ladies, etc., that were popular places of entertainment, but it was nice to see real people who weren't in uniform. Once, a truck hit a mine about half a mile down the road, and we dashed out to help the wounded. It was a little scary as obviously there could have been another mine, or an ambush, waiting for us. But there was no excitement directed toward us.

One of the duties that I was fortunate to miss was the stool-burning detail. It was just luck that I missed it. Because the Cav didn't want any Vietnamese in the camp, we had to burn our own. This was an awful detail; the job was to daily go around to all of the outhouses and get the cut-in-half fifty-five-gallon drums that were used to collect the excrement and then take them to an end of the camp and burn the stool with gasoline. Needless to say, there were never any volunteers for this job. Staying out of trouble had its own advantages.

We had a nice party once because we had traded a large bottle of Darvon capsules with the cooks in exchange for some chicken and steaks, and we proceeded to have our own barbecue. It was always wise to be on the good side of the medics and the cooks. I got a chance to learn some of the slang. The Vietnamese were gooks or slopes or slants, but usually gooks. The enemy was usually called Charlie, short for Victor Charlie, the military phonetic equivalent for V(iet) C(ong). Actually, I'm not certain that there were any real Viet Cong left when I got there, as most of them had been killed during Tet. Certainly, the enemy that we saw were all hard-core North Vietnamese regulars.

A favorite line of my troop was "It don't mean nuthin." This was really a very profound saying. One of the things that you learned quickly was that so many of the things that you had valued before had no value at all in Nam. The only thing that counted was that you got home. There was, of course, the demand that you do your job and protect your buddy, as he was going to protect you. But all the foofaraw about clothes, haircut, music, education, etc. was of no concern. In C Troop, we had a guy who was given the choice of four years in jail or four years in the service. And while I might have been uncomfortable inviting him to come by the house for dinner, in Nam he was a great person because he did his job well and protected your back. One discovered quickly the nitty-gritty of existence and left the dross to the philosophers in the states.

There was a great degree of fatalism in the service. "When my number comes up, I'm going to go." Needless to say, this is all hogwash. In particular, I never saw anyone stand up in the middle of a firefight and say, "Nyay, nyah, you can't hit me. My number hasn't come up yet." But it was easy to understand how they could feel that way as one discovered the capriciousness of war and random chance as your buddies were killed or wounded. Why him and not you? His number came up—what else?

Our medical administrator had a name that rhymed with ding-a-ling, which everyone called him behind his back. He really was a major ding-dong of very doubtful competence. About the best we could say about him was that he wasn't a martinet. On the contrary, he wanted recognition and acceptance very badly. About six months later, one of our medics, doing the night shift in the clinic, happened to be in his office and discovered that he was writing home and describing his exploits by taking them off of the medal citations from the medics who had earned them in the field, where he had never been. This didn't endear him to us any-the-more.

I was really fortunate in one other sense. As we were in camp and had few duties, they allowed me to catch the daily aircraft to Saigon to go to church, as long as I caught the plane back in the afternoon. We had a mission compound in Saigon that was a real godsend to the GIs who were there. I didn't know where it was but I hitchhiked and walked and found it about a mile from the Tan Son Nhut airport. We had Sabbath School and church in English followed by a potluck dinner afterward. It was remarkably refreshing. I met some friends there I had known from teaching at Fort Sam, including one I knew in later life, who lived close to me then, and who became a minister. I met my good friend from basic who had driven me to Waco to get my car (which had broken down). He was a medic in a POW hospital at Long Binh. Of most interest was one of our buddies from basic who hadn't gone on to AIT because he had computer experience (what we had back then). One of his buddies had been assigned to Saigon to the computer center where, among other things, the assignments for incoming GIs were distributed. He spotted his friend's name coming through and pulled it for a spot in Saigon as well. His wife was a nurse, and she came over and worked in a hospital in Saigon as a civilian. About four months later, I got back to Saigon and listened to him complain about how his wife had to work nights and he worked days and it was so terrible that they didn't get together. You just can't imagine how crushed I was to hear of his suffering. Fortunately, I never missed the plane back, and I got to go to Saigon several times, a most blessed interlude even if I never did get to see any of the sights in Saigon.

✝

A JUNGLE SABBATH
A letter home to my father.

You could barely see the sun going down through the monsoon clouds. The noises around you seem strange and unreal. As you look around you see a stark, impressionistic sky and the darkening silhouettes of big monsters of war. Immediately the paradox appears for you are trying to celebrate the beginning of the Sabbath with beauty, horror, life, and death as your roommates.

I'm no one special in Viet-Nam. I see more of the war than some and less than others, but I see a different war than most.

I'm a medic with an armored unit that, unfortunately, spends a great deal of time in the jungle. As each day blends into another the days lose meaning and separation except on the calendar that marks how many days are left until the return home. If anything, the "Sabbath" of the soldier is Monday for it's on Monday that the big, red malaria pill is passed out and it is this that separates one week from another.

So for me, and the rest of us over here, there is a distinct problem in trying to make the Sabbath something special. It's almost impossible to make this a day of rest for even on the Sabbath the job of caring for your men continues.

Each day you ride through jungles from dawn to dusk. Each day you have cuts, bruises, heat casualties, and sometimes the other kind of casualty. Each day you have men depending on you for health and life, whether or not it's the Sabbath.

The routine is the same and the work is the same; what makes the Sabbath special? To me it's usually a state of mind supported by little things. Instead of churches and suits, there is deadly jungle and clothes that haven't been washed for two weeks. The service is what songs you can remember and sing as you scan the brush two feet away. Unfortunately, you can't read the Bible and look at the same time. The Sabbath dinner is the "yummy" C-rations.

This week I was lucky. We had overrun a base camp so we got to stop early. They flew in hot chow, we went bathing in a B52 bomb crater, and after checking my men out there was an opportunity to have a worship service. Normally there's nowhere to go but because it was still light I marked a few feet in front of the vehicles and held my service.

I heard the strange sounds of nature undimmed by harsh engines. With a small breeze, an open Bible and some hymns God once again became something tangible rather than the distant figure one feels but doesn't see during the day.

The paradox of peace at heart and 52-ton behemoths of war impresses more strongly on the mind what a wonderful thing a faith in God really is.

It's sort of funny. Over here everyone combines an attitude of "I believe in God" with "When your time comes, you go." But there is little actual study or attempts to see God. They go through the war trying to forget that they are here rather than trying to get as much as possible from the place, especially in relation to God.

This makes my Sabbath special, even if it is only in my mind. It gives me a chance to concentrate on what He is and to be thankful for what He's given me. His wisdom, faith, and reassurance are irreplaceable for peace of mind. There's no worry about death because I can see a purpose and His guiding hand. I still get scared. My stomach tightens, the muscles quiver and my heart's in my throat. Yet it is the Sabbath, more than at any time, that I know that He's with me.

As the day closes I feel a little empty as if it really isn't a Sabbath, but I think that I understand my Sabbath in a new light. It's not just a day of rest and worship. It's in the heart and soul and mind. It's a peace that is anywhere if it's in you. It's a release, an escape, a comfort, and a blessing. It's a day when all of the trivia and fear are left behind. I don't need a church, a choir, a minister, or any of the normal things. I only need His love and aid.

I don't enjoy it here. I don't enjoy seeing my friends die. Yet I'm thankful too for being here because out here where pride, vanity, and the pleasures of life mean nothing, my God is real. I can feel Him in a different, vital way that others can only guess at. Even death is a more distant thing I can feel and know that I am loved by God. As the theme song of the guy's at our servicemen's center in San Antonio so aptly puts it, "I know the Lord will make a way for me!"

✝

CHAPTER 6

In late February the 1st Squadron took off up the road to our new assignment, with the Sheridans. I had yet to look at a map, so I didn't know where we were going, where we were, or for that matter, where we had been. I still didn't know where Xuan Loc was. We rode on top of the squadron medic track, a large modified command track with extra room inside for minor surgery and what have you, and it was a fascinating trip. For the first ten miles or so, we traveled on dirt roads, and you can imagine what we looked like after a few miles of being fiftieth in the column. It was the first time that I had actually traveled through Vietnam, as opposed to flying over it. You should understand that there are only two seasons in Vietnam, dry and wet. The wet season began in May and June and lasted about four months. This was the season of bottomless mud holes and stuck vehicles. The rest of the year was dry where the holes were now bottomless with dust, and the grit would get in everything. The rice paddies were now dry unless we were near a river where they could irrigate. The people were neither happy nor sad as we passed; rather, they were passive to it all, having seen military columns for as long as most could remember. Every time we stopped, little boys would appear out of nowhere, trying to sell cold sodas, hooch, dirty pictures, watches, or anything else that might be vendible, including time with their putative or real sisters.

Adjusting to their culture took some doing. For instance, in Vietnam, if you wanted to go to the bathroom, you just turned around so that they didn't see your face, and you proceeded to do your business. If you needed to number two, you just turned around and squatted. For the GIs, this usually just meant that if you stopped, all that you did was stand on the side of your track and pee off of the edge. After seven months of that, it was very difficult when I got back to the States to just not pee on the side of the road as I did in Nam. You didn't do some things such as patting children on the head, which was offensive to some religions. All business was transacted with military paper money, which you were paid in, or preferably in Vietnamese money, if you had it. There was a constant struggle in Nam with currency speculators and black marketeers who hoarded money, so every now and then they'd come by and take away all of your money and give you new play money to use. For most of us, it was just a pain in the tush, and most GIs did whatever was the most expedient.

After traveling most of the day, we got to a place about twenty-five miles north of Saigon that the GIs called Holiday Inn because some creative GI had obtained a small Holiday Inn motel sign to decorate the fire base. This was moderately in the sticks and had been occupied off and on before by the Cav, and we were there to protect the 105 mm cannon unit that was there. It had also been overrun before. There was the story, perhaps apocryphal, of a previous doctor who was there when the camp was overrun one night. Apparently, he was totally scared and wouldn't leave his bunker to help out any of the wounded elsewhere during the battle and was promptly transferred a short while later for not doing his job. These stories did nothing to make us feel secure about coming there. Our first job was to fill up sandbags to secure the area. Any combat GI worth his salt will be able to give horror stories about sandbag filling. You didn't want to leave empty bags behind because Charlie could find all sorts of nefarious uses for the bags. Consequently, when you went anywhere, you took your bags with you, emptied from the previous location, and then filled them up again at the new location. You can't imagine how many sandbags it takes to make four walls around a tent, or to make a dugout and then roof it.

As medics at the fire base, we didn't pull guard duty in any of the combat vehicles that guarded the perimeter, so life was moderately easy. I once drove my jeep all the way back to Long Binh to get some supplies that we needed, which was exciting as just the two of us barreled down some empty road wondering where the ambush was. Nobody gave me a map. It was just verbal instructions go down the dirt road to the first paved road and turn right, etc., etc. The good Lord was kind, and we actually made it back up the right road without mishap. Generally, life was fairly boring with not much to do. There was no PX to get reading material, there was just the radio and occasional letters from home. We could get Armed Forces Radio if our batteries weren't dead and the officers would let us. And you had a radio. While at base camp, we had several occasions, once by road and twice by helicopter, to go to some of the neighboring villages for a MEDCAP operation, a kind of medical care for the needy locals' deal. These had been a lot of fun visiting the villages and trying to provide care. Everyone was friendly, at least while we were there, and they provided nice interludes. We occasionally got a horror story back to us of VC coming after we had left and killing off some of the patients, but these took months to filter back to us and took none of the blemish off the operations while we were there. While at Holiday Inn, however, we were on combat operations, even if nothing was happening right then, and couldn't take the chance of not being available if needed. After a few weeks there, the senior medic in C Troop got enough seniority to transfer to the rear, and a new senior medic was named. I was transferred to C Troop to take his place in a combat vehicle platoon.

I joined Charlie Troop in January 1969 and was assigned as the platoon medic for the 3rd Platoon. There were five medics assigned to the troop. There was one for each platoon plus two on the medic track or angel track. This track was basically like every other ACAV in the unit with two M30 machine guns and the fifty-caliber, but it only carried about 2,000 rounds of ammunition with the rest of the space kept clear to carry wounded and litters. This usually followed the captain around, and we only saw it if we were on troop-size functions as opposed to just platoon actions. The senior medic was in charge of the track, and he usually had either the least experienced medic or one of his buddies on the track with him, depending on how he perceived his duty.

In many respects, I was one of the most fortunate of people to be assigned a medic. While I was just as ignorant as most as to what my duties would be, I did get that extra year of teaching under my belt; plus, those extra months in the clinic didn't hurt any. At least I didn't go straight from AIT to the boonies in one jump. I should explain some of the GI slang that was in use. Some made lots of sense; some came from the Vietnamese itself; and some came from fractured French, which was spoken by many Vietnamese. "Boonies" was short for "boondocks." "Toolies" was short for "Tuileries," the palace near Paris, which came out of WWI but which was still somewhat in vogue. To be told by the Vietnamese that you were a "Number One GI" meant that you were "very good," and a "Number Ten GI" was "very bad." "Di Di Mao" (*dee dee maow*), or "Di Di," came from the Vietnamese "go get out of here." "Bookoo" was fractured French for "beaucoup," meaning "many" but often used for "very," as in "bookoo bad GI." "Boomboom" meant "sex," often accompanied by graphic gestures. Because the GIs had money, the Vietnamese became very efficient entrepreneurs at selling to the GIs, often with limited language abilities. Like most cultures, there were those who would milk the system, and more than one GI bought a fine watch to discover that the jewels had been taken out of it and it only ran for a month, or less. On the opposite side of the coin, a modest percentage of GIs really looked down on the Vietnamese as subhuman and would cheat them gladly of anything at the point of a gun. And, as in every war, if you were a sadist to begin with, the war was a natural for you, and you abused anyone who would get in your way, black, white, yellow, or green with purple polka dots.

I was assigned to the troop only hours before they took off, and I threw my gear in the back of the assigned track without knowing anyone, knowing anything about the vehicle, what we did if attacked, etc. Off we went up the road, carefully sitting on the open rear hatch with our legs up. You might wonder why we didn't sit inside where it was "safe" or, at least, stand up while we rode. The real reason is that aluminum alloy doesn't always stop much in the way of weaponry. A powerful rifle, if fired at the right angle, might go through the side. A rocket grenade (RPG) would burn through the side and then hit the other side and explode. This tended to make nasty messes of fleshy things hanging inside the vehicle. Likewise, if we hit a mine, we would probably be thrown off as opposed to thrown around, a fine distinction if it's your body. In a firefight, you stood inside because you wanted a low profile as you hunched behind your machine gun shield and aimed the machine gun. Also, it allowed you to get ammo, spare barrels, hand grenades, smoke grenades, flares, etc. that you might need in a real hurry. As you can imagine, the ride on a mini-tank will never replace a Cadillac's ride. If you could, you had a cushion, but it wasn't always available. Like many things in the service, it depended on your ability to scrounge, beg, borrow, or steal if you were going to be comfortable.

Again, as before, I didn't have the foggiest idea where we were or what we were going to do. In retrospect, I'm not certain that it made much difference. We began a routine that lasted for more than six weeks of going from dawn to dusk, usually in the jungle, trying to get to some position of the map that theoretically contained the enemy. Apparently what happened was that there would be some intelligence somewhere that in such and such a sector there would be a base camp, or something equally as important. They would send us in to find it. We might travel somewhere for part of the day, but usually we would end up "busting jungle" for the rest. To do this, as any enemy worth his salt kept his camps well in the middle of the jungle, we would get a platoon of fifty-two-ton tanks (that's three tanks), and we would divide into three columns, one behind each tank. Then we would begin to knock down the jungle under the big tanks, and we lesser vehicles would follow behind. As you can imagine, traveling over crushed jungle isn't like traveling on a superhighway. We'd be constantly inching over logs, mashed bamboo, gullies, and what have you. I've called vehicles "tracks," which really means any tracked vehicle. It was also our slang word for our ACAVs, and while every vehicle had tracks on it, you could easily throw a track off of an idler wheel if you had some lateral torsion while slipping sideways or if you caught some bamboo in the wheels, etc. This meant that you had to stop, take apart the track with wrenches, manhandle the track into position, and then re-wrench it back together. This was a time-consuming, aggravating chore at best, made worse by heat and sweat and the fear of discovery.

During one operation where everyone was in a hurry, one of the ACAVs threw a track, and the platoon left the rear three of our tracks behind while it was getting fixed. Again there was the acute anxiety of following down some mashed jungle track all alone in the jungle while trying to catch up with the rest. We were, understandably, I think, a little unhappy about being left behind, but apparently the captain was under some pressure to get to some kind of position by a certain time, and he was behind in getting there. That, of course, reassured us not a whit. One of the great truths about being in the armored, as I was to learn very well over the next several months, was that Charlie always knew just where you were. You could take it as gospel that as you made all of these horrendous motor noises while you mashed down the jungle going all of a mile an hour, he knew just where you were. If we went all day and missed him, as we did in that dire emergency above, then the end of another boring day went by. If you discovered something, he knew that we were coming. If he decided that it wasn't worth anything to him, then the camp or whatever was empty. If he decided that he had to fight, or wanted to fight, then he came really prepared. He knew that rifles didn't stop the Cav, he had the rockets ready and waiting for our listening pleasure. We did not feel very secure running around on our own.

We went at least a month of daylong jungle busting before anything exciting happened at all. You should understand the days' activities first. Day began at dawn with any repairs or whatever done early. Morning ablutions, such as they were, were at best cursory. Usually we were on the road/track/path/jungle within thirty minutes. When you awoke, you brought in all the flares and claymore mines that we had set out. You opened some C rations, about which we'll talk later. If you had time and some C-4 explosive was available, you could break off a piece and light it to heat the food. You brushed your teeth, and you might or might not shave. Most only shaved every two or three days. When you started on the track, you re-formed your column and constantly kept looking around you at the jungle or whatever. You should understand that in deep jungle you might only be able to see three feet in front of you, but you kept looking anyway. Radios and other distractions were verboten for the good and logical reason that everyone's life depended on everyone else, and you being a little lazy could mean someone being blown away if you missed something. This was a reasonably strict rule. Once, while on my Sabbath, I was sitting in the middle of the rear hatch reading my Bible. We were traveling down a dirt road in squadron convoy, meaning over a hundred vehicles in column. The jungle had been cleared away from the road by about 150 yards yet our commander flew over in a helicopter and saw me reading my Bible. He radioed to my commander and so on down the line for me to get my act together. Nobody hassled me about it later, but no one wants to irritate the colonel. At any rate, you kept your attention on the jungle for hours until lunch break, which you might or might not get.

If you were on the road, you would eat while traveling. If you were lucky, you got a half-hour break to chow down. Then you started up again until just before sundown. Normally we would then laager up, meaning form into a circle with the nose of the vehicles pointing out and rears inward, set out the flares and mines, make any repairs or vehicle service (at every stop it was checked), organize the guard duty, and heat up food. Any letter writing or other duties got taken care of then. On days that we got resupply, a Chinook helicopter would fly out and bring a hot meal, ammo, water, mail, and any other supplies that we would need. In the morning, we'd start all over again.

Guard duty consisted of divvying up the hours of the night by the number of men in the vehicle. Eight hours of dark meant two hours of guard duty if there were four men in the vehicle. Depending on your seniority, personal preference, etc., you got your slot of time and woke up the next man for his stint. During those two hours, you sat in the cupola behind the fifty-caliber machine gun and stared into the absolute darkness. During the dry season, there might be stars; during the wet season, you often didn't even have that. Occasionally, we had a night scope to use. This was a six-pound, foot long, five-inch-diameter toy that electronically augmented the light that came in and significantly improved how well you could see. But you had to have some light or it wouldn't work. Without stars, you were out of luck. As you can imagine, it got to be very difficult to stay awake while on guard duty. As time wore on and the long hours without breaks added up, you became chronically fatigued and worn down. You were relying on adrenaline every minute of every day, and you'd quit at night. I remember one time about two months before I left Nam when our platoon had become worn down by breakdowns and there were only four vehicles left. They had us pull guard duty in a rubber plantation between two small hills, in the gap between them.

We laagered up in a cross formation, and at about 2:00 a.m., I was really getting dreadfully tired. You tried your darnedest not to make any noise because you never knew who might be somewhere listening, and you wouldn't want to give them a fix on your location. But this time I decided that I had to do something as I was nodding off. So, I got up from the cupola and stood on the side of the vehicle and looked around. I didn't seem to attract any attention from the guy next to me, so I walked over to his vehicle, and he was sound asleep. For that matter, so were the other two guys. This made the delightful situation of three out of four guys on guard being asleep, and the one guy who was awake wouldn't shoot. It wasn't what I would have called an ideal situation. Guys would do all sorts of things to stay awake, including pill popping, and they'd try to get stimulants from me. Usually I wouldn't do it because I didn't have many to start with, and I knew that sooner or later they'd pay for it with other problems. Guys would smoke, which really irritated me because Charlie can smell smoke a long ways away; they'd masturbate, dream weird fantasies, do isometric exercises, etc. just to try and keep their eyes open.

You may recall that in basic training I wouldn't train with weapons. We got harassed relatively frequently by other GIs about what we'd do in combat, and usually we'd say we didn't know. We'd just do the best we could. God would be with us, etc. They'd come up with all sorts of fanciful situations that you could be found in, and sometimes they'd get pretty snooty. Some of the sergeants could get nasty and insult your manhood, patriotism, etc. When I got to Nam, they asked us once about weapons, and I declined, about the second day that I was at Blackhorse. They made it clear that I could change my mind whenever I wanted, but they never harassed me officially after that. Now, you may be asking yourself why they had a medic who wouldn't shoot standing guard. It began that way initially because I was a warm body. Everyone knew that I wouldn't carry a weapon, but they let it ride. Up until about one month before I left

Nam. We were in a troop formation laagered up around a building, and there had been some activity in the area. I was on guard and had the starlight scope when, for the first and only time I was in Nam, lo and behold, I saw something through the scope. I wasn't sure, but it looked like two Vietnamese carrying rifles and walking down the road about seventy-five yards in front of us. There were claymore mines attached to the cupola that I could have blown off, but I wouldn't do it. I didn't even know enough to be certain that they were NVA, although I confess that they probably were, but I couldn't get anybody's attention, and by the time someone was alerted, they were gone. After that, Top, the top sergeant, decided that they really didn't need a guard like me after all. Part of me felt bad, but I sure did enjoy the extra sleep.

I settled into the routine pretty quickly, not that there were many options. Every evening I'd go around and give everyone a vitamin pill and malaria pill if available. I'd walk around and find out who was hurting. There were a variety of aches and pains, and we had a small assortment of medicine, including antibiotics that we dished out as wisely as we could, especially considering that we had had almost no training in drug use. I was the guy who decided if someone was sick enough that they had to see a doctor, but that wasn't too often. There were always insect bites and the infrequent scorpion bites from GIs who weren't careful to check their boots or blankets before they were used. It wasn't unusual to have an assortment of bumps, bruises, and scrapes because as the jungle got mashed down, vines would occasionally get caught in the tracks of a vehicle and would get pulled down with a crash. My first casualty on an operation occurred a couple of weeks after I joined the unit as we were busting jungle. I got a call to go up front, and a tank commander had been injured by a tree that had gotten pulled down from behind by a vine. It came crashing down on his head and knocked him down onto the tank. Commanders wear helmets, but as I started breathing mouth-to-mouth, I could feel the bones in the back of his head crunch underneath my hands. It was an awful sensation made worse by his vomit and blood in his mouth and nose. We tried for over half an hour without any luck, and eventually the troop knocked down enough trees for a helicopter to come in and take him out. It was particularly awful as he was well liked and had only two more weeks to go in-country. His wedding was to take place one week after that. It set an awful pall over the whole troop, and I was in tears over my failure to keep him alive.

Overlooking Cambodia from a hill near Loc Ninh.

**The tank commander is overlooking the Montagnard village.
While the Montagnards were normally our allies',
one could never be totally sure of anything.**

**Any time we stopped the vehicles got checked.
If there are kids around you're almost always safe.**

**The Sheridan weighed only about 17 tons
but it didn't have a big tank motor to push through the bamboo.
We had to back out and go around.**

Usually we traveled in three columns and busted jungle.
Columns allowed us to rapidly spread out our fire power
to the sides as well as forward.

When the whole regiment moved it made for a very long column and
there were strict rules for distance between vehicles, travel speed, etc.

We're traveling on a work road in old rubber trees.
The irregulars worked with the Special Forces.

Each small town had their own little market, if only a couple of houses.

Any stop created time for servicing your track. Besides the engines
one would look at the tracks, the idler wheels, track tension, and so on.

In the monsoon season if you got a break you tried to clean out the mud
and dry everything out. Rusty (on the left) was my best medic. Unfortunately
I've forgotten the name of the other medic. He was new but also a nice guy.
He had trouble learning just as I did.

I've lost both of their names. The track commander was a southern boy who liked to play cards after payday. They'd get in a track and then closed it up while they played poker. Usually the lifers walked away with the money.

This is the track that I got off of a few minutes before.
Bob Dickson (cleaned up) was the track commander.

Any kind of base, no matter how small, would have a berm around it with rows of barbed wire outside. There could also be mines, trip flares, cans of stones hanging on the wire, etc.

A Thunder Run was a very fast run to an emergency or a new location.

This is a "Long Tom" 175 mm cannon that provided long distance fire support for surrounding troops.

This is a POL stop (Petroleum, Oil, Lubricants).
This was at Lai Khe before we started North again.

The Cav was sent to Nam, in part, to see if armor could function in monsoon seasons. The heavy tanks at monsoon time would get stuck in the paddy's, whereas our lighter Cav vehicles might get through. Usually we avoided them.

If the Colonel wants you to go somewhere you try. Here we were blocked by a small river. We could get down one side but it was too steep to get up the other side. The bridge was too old and light weighted to support our vehicles. So we cruised down the river until we could find a place to get up the other side. The fact that there were a bunch of kids there was reassuring.

I opened a case of C-Rats labeled 1953. I couldn't tell the difference.
These guys are just lucky that they got a break to heat up the rations
with bits of C4 explosives.

We not only got the new Sheridan's in January, we got other new ACAV's as well.

There was a 105 mm cannon battery at the fire base and someone got flags from all of the states that had a Holiday Inn, 26 at the time. They built their club from the used, wooden ammunition boxes.

As can be imagined many people in combat turned to God. The Catholic priests in wartime were often some of their best, as noted by the many awards and Medals of Honor, that the priests received during the war.

The rubber trees with their long rows made it a great place for maneuvering tracks or firing long distances.

This one time we had a Seas of Grass that allowed us to spread out and cover large areas as we moved ahead.

Captain West was our troop commander during most of my time with the Cav.

While tracks could go many places it still took good driving skills.
If you got stuck you might need an M88 tank retriever to pull you out
or else a heavy lifting helicopter.

We held the top and bottom, the enemy had the whole middle.
At night you could see flares and contact at the top.
The mountain stood all by itself in the middle of the jungle.

Often different units of the Cav would be sent in to examine where the B52's had dropped their loads. A big crater could hold a whole tank.

A classic stop in a Ville. The kids immediately came out to
sell sodas, beer, watches, or anything else they could get you.
Vietnamese alcoholic drinks were definitely an acquired taste.
Giving the kids candy or gum was always a hit.

Smoke was used to mark your position in the jungle for helicopters and airplanes to see your position. Making certain that the aircraft knew which color smoke was yours was mandatory in any fight.

Jesse Davenport show his fatigue and sartorial splendor
while riding in the Blackhorse.

Sgt. Bates came to us halfway through my tour and
was one of the platoon leaders.

Danny lost track of his best friend who was wounded and he thought that he was dead. He found him about 35 years later and they stayed best friends until Danny died a few years ago.

We always wore flak jackets but it was way too hot and humid to keep them zipped up. I wore the scissors but it was easy to bend over and lose them so I bought a nice knife in Hawaii while on R&R. You kept your hair short due to the climate and the lack of barbers.

We're stopped at Thunder 4 - 4 small sites from previous trips up the road to Loc Ninh. We laagered up there. Beauty can be found anywhere but you can never forget the war.

CHAPTER 7

We had the briefest of in-country combat courses while at the Blackhorse. While I personally didn't get a weapon, I went out to the range, and I wandered around while the other guys were sighting in their M16s. There were no faked, or real, booby-trapped trails to go down, nor any special courses or lectures. They did give people a chance to throw some live hand grenades, an exercise that was livened up a lot by the nincompoopery of one of the GIs who couldn't throw a Willie Pete over a berm five yards away.

A berm, for the uninitiated, is a large dirt wall, in our cases usually about ten feet high. We had a large berm around our whole camp. The berm was topped by razor concertina wire, a fancy intermingled barbed wire that came in four-foot diameter rolls, which was held in place by stakes. In front of the berm, about thirty yards away over cleared ground was a stack of one roll on two rolls of more concertina. There were two similar stacks at thirty-yard intervals in front of that. Plus, there was an assortment of mines, trip flares, and the like intermingled with the mess. The field of fire was a reasonably imposing setup to try and protect you. Further, there were guard towers with machine guns at various sites around the berm. Nevertheless, it was once demonstrated, by a Kit Carson scout, a VC defector, how easily a trained man could cross under the contraption in less that a minute without setting off a single booby trap. Obviously, it was important to be able to throw a hand grenade over the berm. Willie Peter, an old army slang for the letters "W" and "P," stood for "white phosphorus" (WP). This is a particularly nasty substance that explodes in a large white puff that sprays this phosphorus over a wide area. Phosphorus, on contact with air, burns, and if it gets on the skin, the only way to keep it from burning through you is to dig it out or to cover it completely with something to keep the oxygen totally shut out from the phosphorus. Anyway, this booby only threw the grenade about fifteen feet and hit the near side of the berm, and the grenade promptly started rolling back. It's an exercise in humility to see how fast the human body can move under the right stimulation. Fortunately, no one was hurt.

I went through that whole mess so that you would understand that I didn't have the foggiest idea what enemy weapons sounded like. I only had a vague idea what our weapons sounded like. One didn't go shooting at things much—it was really frowned on—because immediately everyone went bonkers shooting into the jungle, etc. because no one wanted Charlie to get the first shot. In fact, we had a specific routine called, euphemistically, reconnaissance by fire, where we would all start firing into the jungle if we thought that Charlie might be there. This in an attempt to try and keep him from getting the first shot and disrupting our fighting and planning. Again, you should understand that you couldn't see three feet into the jungle, so you had to guess if someone was there. The routine was that you fired in short bursts so as to not overheat the barrel of the gun and to try and put one round into every square foot in front of you, starting in close and weaving back and forth from up close to far away, and then start again. The idea being that if Charlie was out there, at least this way you could keep his head down. If he wouldn't look, he couldn't fire at you very well.

Toward the end of April, we had been hustling for over a month, most of the time in an area north of Saigon that had been called the Iron Triangle. This area had been exclusively Charlie's until recently and we were delegated the chore of trying to remove the remaining hangers-on, clear out bunkers, etc. Charlie was remarkably creative in making his camps. He was always very well camouflaged, usually using living vines and plants to hide everything. He most often dug into the ground, and the stories of underground bunkers that might go for miles are legion, as are the stories of their booby traps. Tunnel rats were special super gung-ho GIs who specialized in going into tunnels to check them out. This was so dangerous that frequently only volunteers were allowed the chore. It was certainly true that it took a certain special kind of nerve—either courage or lunacy as you will—to be a tunnel rat. The bunkers, when close to the surface, would be covered by layers of three-inch branches or the like in a crossing pattern and covered by layers of dirt and growth of vine, etc. There would usually be a small hole at ground level that you could look out of that was, of course, camouflaged by ground cover. It could be remarkably difficult to see that gun slit and very difficult to destroy the bunker. In one fight that I remember, one of our tanks had fired at least two 152 mm high explosive rounds into the bunker and only left a hole the diameter of your arm in the top of the bunker. By firing in a pattern to cover all of the ground in the firefight, you hoped to put a bullet into that space even if you couldn't see it. Needless to say, destroying the bunkers, and those in it, was a high priority.

Napalm, or jellied gasoline, was a terrible and lovely weapon. The gasoline would flow across the ground and into the holes and crevices. If it didn't destroy Charlie, it would either burn up the oxygen or force him to leave. There's no question that it was a terribly destructive weapon that did evil things, and as a noncombatant, I wasn't pleased much, but there was no way that I could ever side with the creeps who were demonstrating in the USA that it was inhumane and shouldn't be used. I would have been thrilled to have stopped the war, but if it had to be fought, I certainly believed that my men and I deserved every chance we had to be alive. As George Patton once said, roughly, "You're here to make the other soldier die for *his* country." If that napalm killed one "gook" and it saved the life of my buddy, then it was worth it. Many GIs protested the war; not many protested the weapons. And darn few wanted anything until their sons and brothers came home. Almost no one who had actually been fighting hated napalm. You should also appreciate that only 10 percent of the GIs who made it to Nam actually did any fighting. The rest were just in support. Now, it was certainly true that death could find you anytime or anywhere. That cute little shoeshine boy you gave candy to could slip a hand grenade in your gas tank and blow you up without batting an eye. Your truck could hit a mine. Your camp could be mortared, and by luck you'd get hit. You could catch some dumb disease and die. But only 10 percent actually went out fighting, and this has been true all the way back to the Revolutionary War. The rest pushed supplies, or papers, ran clubs, repaired vehicles, worked in hospitals, etc.

Once we got them out of the bunkers, then what. We certainly didn't want to give them back as soon as we moved out. A whole bunch of things were tried. Water was pumped in them, but it just got absorbed by the ground. If they were small, we might blow them up with C4. We could use artillery, but that wasn't very efficient, although B52s with 10,000-pound bombs did neat things to bunkers. Often we exploded variations of tear gas in the bunkers that would lay dormant there for months until someone would come walking through and stir everything up. It was a constant problem for which I don't think anyone ever had a really good answer. Probably the best was that once the camp had been found, Charlie didn't want it much, as he could never be certain that we might not come back to check up on it. At any rate, our usual day-to-today chore was looking for bunker complexes. We'd often overrun them, literally, and notice them afterward, the holes were that well camouflaged. Plus, you could never trust intelligence to know what they were doing, so you had to work on the assumption that there might be other bunkers around that they didn't know about, or the bunkers might be in another spot. Consequently, one was always anxious that something might occur, and it would be sudden when it did.

I had settled in pretty well by the end of April, but some things were still in the air. The people accepted that I wasn't going to carry a weapon, even if they didn't understand it, but until I had proved myself, the jury was still out on me as a person. The 29th of April was a typical hot day busting jungle, and I was in the last vehicle of the middle of three columns. About nine in the morning, I heard some firing up front, but it sounded like reconnaissance by fire. My track commander turned around after a while and yelled at me that someone was hurt up front, so I grabbed my aid bag and went forward semi-hurrying over that uneven mashed-down bamboo and vines. As I got up front, everything was chaotically noisy with the vehicles up front being spread out into a semicircle with every weapon firing. I'd never seen that before, but there were loads of things that I'd never seen, and this wasn't all that strange. No one was paying attention to me, nor could I see anyone hurt or needing help. Everybody on the tracks and tanks were looking the other way. I couldn't get anyone's attention. Finally, I wandered up front beside the front of an M48 tank and waved my hands until the tank commander looked down to the side. With a considerable look of astonishment, he finally figured out what I wanted and pointed to another tank over on the other side behind the others. I went boogying over to that tank and finally figured how to crawl up on the side as no one was around to give me any clues, and those are big tanks. I'd seen them before, but I'd never had to crawl up on one, or thought that I'd have to. I finally got to the top and looked inside, and there was a wounded person at the bottom with a medic next to him. There was absolutely no room for me in there, and it was loud enough that he couldn't hear me yell, so I stood around for a while wondering what to do. Finally, I crawled down the outside and stood by the side, figuring they would call me when they wanted me. My platoon hadn't appeared yet. This whole process had taken ten to fifteen minutes, and as I stood there like some kind of idiot, I saw a rocket explode against the side of a tank.

Now, I might have been ignorant of what was happening, but by the end of the day, I qualified as an expert at recognizing what enemy rockets and rifles sounded like when fired, to say nothing about what our machine guns, etc. sounded like. My mother's little boy wasn't a total fool, and you'd better believe that I started in the practice of keeping a low profile. The medic track came up, and we unloaded the wounded man, and a long, hot day began.

Needless to say, I didn't keep a diary of the day or an hour-by-hour log of what was happening; life was a bit too frantic for that. Much of the time I did nothing other than try to keep out of the way. You'd hear about a casualty, and you'd go there and try to help; then you'd wander back to your platoon. We didn't have lots of casualties, as we were a good unit, but it was difficult to treat them when you had them. The tracks, in order to make a more difficult target, would rock back and forth about ten feet, and you'd have to try and jump on the back of the moving track to get on. Needless to say, one didn't want to walk around the front to try and get in. The back door was too small to use and often blocked up by cans and gear while the vehicle was rocking back and forth, and there was the very real possibility that you could get run over in the confusion. Once inside, you'd be crouching inside a hot, sweaty, stinking vehicle that was rocking back and forth with the guns still blaring while you tried to find the injury and patch it up. Often you only needed the field dressings that you had, but you sometimes had to be creative to cover a large wound or a wound in a funny place. Then, if it wasn't too bad, you left him there or else tried to evacuate him, preferably by walking. Nobody wanted to stop the vehicle, let down the back gate, and take a bunch of people to move a wounded person in the middle of a fight unless it was absolutely necessary. If you could leave the guy, you then got back up in the open space, looked around for who needed you, and tried to hop off the still backing and filling track. I got a pretty fair burn on one arm while trying to get up on the back of a track. To do this, you timed a jump with the coming back roll of the track, planted the foot on a down-slanted place on the bottom left or right of the track, and then jumped up before you slipped off. You then reached over the hatch with a long arm to grab the inside of the hatch and pulled yourself up. But as I reached over the top, which I couldn't see, I reached over a red-hot fifty-caliber machine gun barrel that had been switched off with a new barrel because the first was red-hot.

The day went on endlessly. Sometimes you'd have to escort a wounded person to the back as the medic track didn't stay up front. It was difficult to get help, as you didn't want to crawl around on the fronts of tracks to get a commander's attention, looking for help. You wanted them to fight, and they wanted you out of the way, unless it was necessary. They had their job, and you had yours. Besides, having learned, finally, that I made a large target, there was no way that I was going to expose that body unless necessary. All the movie pictures of crawling around in the jungle were worthless in this kind of fight. Number one, the jungle was all mashed down. Number two, you could get run over while crawling on the ground; no one would see you. Number three, it would take forever to get anywhere. Consequently, you ran hunched over as fast as you could, which got slower and slower as the day went on. By the end of the day, and three or more canteens of water later, walking was the best I was going to do. While I didn't have a rifle, I did have a flak jacket, pot helmet, aid bag, and assorted other gear that I had to manipulate and carry around. Speaking of which, after a while, all of the medics junked their M16s as well; they were just in the way, and no one used them anyway. We almost never had more than two people to manhandle a litter around, and there just wasn't any way that we could run while carrying one of those litters over that mashed jungle. Those fancy war movies where the hero just picks up the wounded man and goes jogging off are pretty fancy. It takes a really good man to pick up a two-hundred-pound man, plus his gear, as dead weight and walk off with him.

You should understand one thing about combat. It is total chaos. You are surrounded by 360-degree noise—all loud. The tracks are rocking back and forth with gear changes, accelerating and so on. All the guns are going off—on all sides of you. There is yelling and screaming and explosions. Tank turrets may blow up seventy-five feet into the air, and you're praying that they don't come down and hit you. RPGs are going off. Then you had to throw in the odors. You had engine exhaust, vomiting, blood, sweat, etc. On top of that, your focus is no more than fifteen feet wide in front of you. Someone ten feet away will have a totally different memory of what was happening. As a medic, you were running from place to place, always trying to get back to your boys, and occasionally lost. By the end of the day, you were exhausted. The gun sounds were so loud that by the end of the day, both ears were hurting, and I had to try walking/running to get over the trees and bamboo with my fingers in my ears. You had to yell for me to understand you.

In the early afternoon, I noticed one of the tracks being "dead" on the front line. It was smoking some as an RPG had gone off inside and there was a small telltale hole on the side. It was in a different platoon than mine, so I didn't pay too much attention at first, but then I noticed someone slouched over in the cupola. I went to the senior medic and asked him about the injured man, and he said that he was dead. I asked if he was sure, and he said he was, so I ignored him and returned to my platoon. I'm angry about myself to this day as several hours later, as the fight passed them by and someone checked him out, we discovered that he was still alive. Now, I was perfectly willing to risk my life for our men, but it seemed silly to risk it for a dead man. The only way to have gotten him out would have been to stand straight up on the front of the track and lift him up out of the cupola, not something recommended for people who don't like holes in their body. And certainly not something to do for a dead man. Likewise, the track was smoking; who knows what might have gone off inside if someone were in there. But if he had said that he didn't know how bad he was hurt, I could have at least checked, whether or not the senior medic wanted to risk his life. I hope that trooper lived because my conscience has bothered me ever since. You may rest assured that I never trusted *anything* that that senior medic ever told me in the future. I still can't believe he did that.

Toward the late afternoon they called in an air strike, and some F105s came by and laid down some ordinance on the bunker line to our right front. The routine was that we threw out colored-smoke canisters to our front. The pilots then told us what color smoke was there and agreed if it was ours. We had learned that if the planes called for red smoke, Charlie might be listening, and he would also throw out red smoke. This way he didn't get a chance to interfere. We were told the planes were coming, and everyone was supposed to keep his head down, but one of my troopers apparently didn't get down, or else he picked up a wound from the enemy, but at any rate he picked up a hole in the left side of his head just below the helmet. He was a loader on one of the Sheridans, so we hustled over and manhandled him out of the tank. We actually got four of us to carry his litter—only one was a medic—and we were hurrying back as best we could when a handle pulled out of the litter, and he went crashing down. We were all feeling really bad as "Slim" was a special guy, and it looked like he was dead, and that that happened seemed the final degradation. He was probably our last casualty as Charlie's resistance started slowing down after the air force came in.

By about 7:00 p.m., we pulled back a ways and laagered up and got some ammo. We grabbed chow as best we could because there was an enormous amount of work to do. Tracks needed maintenance, barrels had to be changed, ammo inventoried and replaced. We hadn't run out, but we were getting low. It's a heck of a fight that will blow our quantity of ammunition. I had made out tags for all of the wounded to be sent along with them, and this had to be sorted out; plus, I went around to see how everyone else was doing. I made out a tag for me. While I didn't tell anyone and didn't have any intention of going to the rear, I wanted to be sure that if someday I needed some kind of plastic surgery or something for my arm, at least the army had a record that it had happened in the service, and not after I got out of the service. I discovered that I had some bits of shrapnel in my face, and I hadn't any idea where they had come from, but nothing else was wrong. Overall, I was pleased with my platoon, and while fearful for the morrow, I at least felt some confidence that I wouldn't do anything too stupid.

The next morning, we went back in, but there was no resistance at all. We discovered that we had overrun a battalion hospital. There were French dressings and IVs around. There were some rooms that were probably surgery rooms. Most of the stuff had been cleared out, but it was fascinating to look around. There were walks under camouflage that had been pulled over from the bushes on the sides of the trail to form a living canopy, with seats for the wounded to sit on. I'd have loved to have spent some time going through the complex. Of course, the poo-bahs all came flocking to see the loot, weapons, etc. Lots of pictures were taken, although not of the guys who captured it. The upshot was the next day we were off again. I had had my baptism by fire, and no one ever hinted that I wasn't welcome because I didn't carry a weapon. I had done my job and backed up my guys, and that was what counted. Only once during my stay in Nam did it ever come up again, and that's a later story.

CHAPTER 8

Following our brief rest, we got back on the road and drove down south almost to Saigon, and then we headed back north again but on a more westward highway. We never did get any idea as to what was going on with the unit, to say nothing of the Cav as a whole. I guess that the officers knew, but it was never filtered down to us lowly bums. We headed up into Tay Ninh province, which was northwest of Saigon and projected like a beak into Cambodia. We got almost as far as the city of Tay Ninh when we turned back into the bush and headed east into the wastes west of where we had been before. This land was considerably flatter and with a different type of jungle. Here we hit patches of thicker bamboo and one time hit a patch of particularly thick bamboo, thicker than your thigh, that was so bad that the M48s couldn't bust through it, and we ended up backing up and going around the mess.

We passed close to the mountain of Nui Ba Den, translated as Black Virgin Mountain, which was a moderately high mountain of a couple of thousand feet that stuck up all by itself right in the middle of a flat plain. There was a small outpost at the top that we were told was held by some Green Berets and which was frequently the source of a lot of attention by the NVA. The summit made a great place for observing the whole plain, and consequently it was frequently attacked. During the daytime, you could fly in or out, but the sides of the mountain were Charlie's, and at night you did what they wanted, not what you wanted. We couldn't always see the mountain due to the jungle, but I would swear that at least half the nights we could see flares going off on the mountain. It again showed those who were under constant stress and combat. We were under constant stress, but combat was infrequent. Many had nothing but stress, the constant worry when they were going to be overrun. There were loads of stories about Charlie's skills and semi-invincibility. There's no question that they had good discipline and many good skills. Nevertheless, they weren't even remotely invincible. They just didn't allow any half-baked jobs. There was only a little room for error. Most GIs had only a little stress at any time, if at all, other than not being home and having limited entertainment facilities.

We were frequently moved around as part of a big chess board. We would be put in position to block the escape of someone escaping away from another unit. This always struck me as dumb because I assumed that they always knew where we were. Yet in fact, they did sometimes run into us, or rather, into our sister units. They weren't all-knowing. I felt particularly insecure in one of our positions because we had been put on the end of a little trail that was surrounded by marsh that wouldn't have supported any of our vehicles. There was only the one trail out, and we'd have been in trouble if they'd ambushed us. On one of these excursions, we were in an area where B52s had dropped their bombs, and there were some large craters. As we were in early rainy season, these were filled with water. At one of our stops, we were in position early and had some extra time. So the boys threw some grenades into the bomb craters to kill anything that was there, and everyone piled in to take a bath and swim a little. It was a lot of fun with a fair bit of roughhousing until a practical joker started firing into some trees. There was nothing there, but no one else knew it, and there was great laughter watching everyone skedaddle as fast as possible to get dressed.

We gradually worked our way south without any particular incidents and finally broke out into a rubber plantation near Cu Chi, a large city about halfway between Saigon and Tay Ninh. While there, we had a little fun. One of our guys had gotten hepatitis, and it fell to me to give everyone a gamma globulin shot in the rear. Gamma globulin is given to give short-term protection against hepatitis and has the rough consistency and appearance of Kayro syrup. It is a moderately painful injection, and there were many ribald comments about sore bottoms. Fortunately, no one else got sick, no doubt because of my needling so many butts. I haven't been that big a pain in the butt since, honest.

My religious experience had its ups and downs. There's an old saying that there are no atheists in foxholes. There's some truth to that. As you became more convinced of your mortality, you could become very devout. I tried hard to read my Bible daily and felt pretty confident about my relationship with God. That didn't mean that I wanted to die or even totally felt ready to die; it did mean that I knew that God existed and that we had a relationship together. If I died, I knew that I wanted to be with him and felt that he wanted me to be with him as well. My Sabbaths, while externally no different from any other day, remained special. Although I remember one week when I had a particularly good Sabbath and one week later I got to the end of the Sabbath day before I remembered that it even was the Sabbath. The days just ran together, and I had lost track. I didn't do much in the way of proselytizing, partly because I didn't have any papers or tracts to use, partly because of the difficulty of finding time to talk, and partly because of my own insecurities. Yet there was plenty about me that was different to cause questions to be asked. For instance, I didn't drink or curse and really was different from the average GI.

We had occasional GIs come back from R&R who caused some comment. Every GI who stayed in-country for a year got a five-to-six-day R&R in a foreign city. "R&R" meant "rest and recreation," or some variation of same, such as "rousing and rutting." The government transported you both ways, but your entertainment was your own. You had to request where you wanted to go, which didn't mean that you'd get it, and then you'd get your orders for your vacation. There were several different sites. Married men could go to Honolulu, and single men usually got sent to other sites, such as Tokyo, Hong Kong, Bangkok, Sydney, or Kuala Lampur in Malaya. Sydney was popular because they had round-eyed women and spoke in English. If you wanted more exotic entertainment, it was easier to find in the more Asian cities. I did get one guy who was running a 104-degree temperature. I felt certain that he had malaria, but he was refusing to do anything about it because he had his R&R coming up in Hawaii with his wife. Finally, he was so sick that he couldn't function, and we shipped him back. One of my great frustrations was that I almost never heard what happened to my guys who got sent back, whether wounded or sick. Unless they came back, it was if they had never existed.

The rainy season made life more miserable. However much we hated the dust, you could get lost in the mud. You were constantly getting wet and then drying out in the heat. You'd do all sorts of shenanigans to protect your gear from mildewing. I kept my Bible and wallet in two separate plastic bags to keep them dry. Condoms were popular to keep rolled socks in. We weren't allowed to close the hatch at night because of the chance of emergency, so we'd string a poncho over the top. When on guard, you'd huddle in another poncho draped over the cupola. The monsoons would sweep through in brief, very hard rains that would leave everything soaked. You'd try to dry out in the steaming, humid heat afterward, and then hours later, you'd get hit again. You could get really cold in Nam. No one had field jackets to stay warm or dry; they were much too heavy. But you could be working in 110-degree jungle heat, get hit with a downpour as the sun was going down, and have the temperature drop forty or more degrees really fast, plenty enough to make you pretty cold. There were some lightweight blankets for us, if you were lucky enough to have one, but your soaked clothes didn't help a bit. Plus, everyone would be sleeping inside the track if at all possible, which made for cramped, stinky sleep at best.

Food continued to be C rations unless we were lucky to get re-supplied when they'd try to bring in a hot meal in some thermos containers. Even then it wasn't always very good. Reconstituted milk just doesn't taste real, and reconstituted ice cream, the few times that we got any, just plain stank. Reconstituted eggs can't have been much better than they were in WWII. The water was thoroughly purified with more chlorine than they put in US swimming pools. You'd try most anything to change the taste of the water. Sugar would just melt, but you'd get presweetened lemonade at the PX, if by chance you got near a PX. I can't stand artificial sweeteners to this day because of too much of that junk in Nam. If we got resupplied, we often got a ration of sodas, and rarely beer. If we were really lucky, we got some blocks of ice with it, and we could roll our sodas. By rolling your can quickly on the block of ice, you could cool it very quickly and get an ice-cold soda very quickly. It was heavenly, if infrequent.

We worked with GIs from the 1st Air Cav several times. They had the reputation of being tough GIs, about which I can't comment, but they daily got resupplied by their choppers, and each GI got beer and sodas daily. They might have been tough, but they were living better than we were. If we were lucky, we might go on an operation with some GIs from another unit that we occasionally hauled around and had the new freeze-dried rations that were highly prized by us when available. I suspect that they got tired of those rations also, but they were delightful compared to fifteen-year-old Cs. An occasional treat was a large can of peanut butter. This still had the oil on top, which was stirred in with a large spoon. I dislike peanut butter to this day.

There was one interlude of some note. My twin sister, who had been teaching school in Beirut, Lebanon, was going to come home to the States through the Orient and scheduled her plane trip through Hong Kong to Saigon. Through the kindness of my commander, I was allowed to hop a supply chopper into Saigon that Sabbath and met her at the mission compound. We had a really good time together, but I had to catch the chopper back that afternoon and fortunately didn't miss anything of significance. My sister had an extra day and with a friend hitched a ride on a helicopter to Vung Tau, a resort on the China Sea, and had a great time. I must admit, whatever I might have thought about my commanders, they certainly were good to me.

After this stint, we got sent to Long Binh to work on our vehicles. They tended to get beat up over time with all of the banging around, busting jungle, absence of service, and so on. Base camp commanders didn't like combat troops in general. We were more boisterous, less tolerant of beaurocratic nonsense, didn't dress as well, drank too much, and in general were troublemakers because we weren't under their thumb. Consequently, they put our troop on a small square of asphalt at least half a mile from the nearest anything. Immediately upon our arrival, they told us that we were restricted and couldn't go anywhere. Now, this did not go over very well. We had long since used up many basic supplies such as stationery, shaving gear, hot sauce for Cs, adulterants for the water, and so on. To say nothing about the dreamed of chance of hitting a bar and getting smashed. This was, of course, a totally dangerous idea. I mean, who knew what trouble we roughnecks would cause. Perish the thought, we might even have a good time, but more likely we would contaminate the good boys who lived and worked on the base.

A delegation of half a dozen guys went to the PX and got supplies, and they arranged for some beer to be brought out, so it wasn't too bad. The first time the crew went out, they got into trouble by just walking down the road. The base commander, a bird colonel, just happened to see them walking by. They probably only gave a half-hearted salute, if that, as we didn't do any saluting in the boonies. After all, none of our officers wanted to label themselves as an officer. He came roaring back and saw their grungy, unwashed clothes, their unpolished boots, the absence of insignia, name tags, or rank, their sloppy slouch hats, and their totally unmilitary appearance and promptly had a cow and began reaming them out. He proceeded to march them back and yelled at our captain a while, receiving the dutiful "yessirs," "nossirs." After the colonel left, the captain just cautioned the boys to take a different route and salute a little faster. After all, there wasn't anything the boys could do about their clothes anyway; it was the best they had. One of our tanks got pulled over by an MP in a jeep, red light spinning. He was blamed for speeding around the perimeter road. I don't recall what the speed limit was—pretty slow, I'm sure—but our boys were used to going full out. If you were traveling anywhere, you didn't dawdle if it could be helped. Slow vehicles made good targets. I doubt that our boys were going too fast, but that didn't mean much to the MPs as they tried to stop a fifty-two-ton tank while riding in their jeep. Bureaucrats just have no sense of humor anyway.

They gave me a pretty lax rein as my duties were somewhat limited, not having to repair any tracks. Not that I knew what to do anyway. I got a chance to go to the POW hospital compound where Dan worked, which was interesting. We had known each other at college. I couldn't go in, but his stories about the POWs were fascinating. Most wonderful miracle of all, I got to use their shower, complete with hot water, and the special miracle of all: a flush toilet. While life there must have been boring and confining, it wasn't very difficult. They had Vietnamese ladies who came in and did all of the cleaning, all of the laundry, all of the shoe polishing, and all of the scut work. This for a very modest sum of money, which no one begrudged. Most of the house ladies were uglier than sin, and who knew how many were VC, but the thought of having to do their own chores was anathema. At night it was strictly verboten for any Vietnamese to be in the camp, but every few weeks some ambulance or truck would get inspected, and they'd find some ladies of the night who had been there for the night. Boys will be boys after all.

We had about a week there, and I got to go into Saigon again for church, which was nice. This time I hitchhiked back and forth without too much trouble, and it was a good drive, and it was nice to see the city, even if it wasn't much of the city. I still hadn't seen any sights, and never did, for that matter, but you did get a different perspective as opposed to flying into Tan Son Nhut. After everything was shipshape, or as much as could be, we headed back north again toward An Loc.

CHAPTER 9

Shortly after the big fight we moved out of the jungle and began a relatively short trip to the town of An Loc, where we could do some repairs for our vehicles. An Loc was a lovely town on the highway due north of Saigon halfway to Cambodia. There were some small industries dealing with the local rubber plantations as well as a market and so on. It was fortified for protection against the NVA, but there wasn't any room for us in the town; rather, we went through the town and about two miles east of town, we made camp on the side of the road in a rubber plantation. The rubber plantations were owned by the French inhabitants and the big rubber corporations, in particular Michelin, who used it in tires, etc. No doubt many of them paid off the NVA to leave them alone and continue commerce in spite of the war but ostensibly they were on our side and anti-Communist.

The plantations were designed with rubber trees planted in straight rows ten meters, roughly thirty-three feet, apart. As the trees were placed in even rows, you could look for long distances between the trees as the trees followed long straight lines. This spacing left room for the trees to grow, and the ground between the trees was kept clean of undergrowth so as not to inhibit the growth of the trees. On hills there might be transverse ditches between the rows of trees to channel any runoff of water and prevent erosion; otherwise, it was flat in each direction. This made for great tank country as we could travel pretty quickly through the trees. Each tree was tapped with twisting descending lines going around the bole of tree, and each year the line would be recut into the bark a little higher. Eventually the lines would take up too much space and the tree couldn't be used, but that wasn't too common as it took a long time to cut all of those lines. There would be nice dirt roads that would wind around the plantations for the small trucks that would collect the rubber sap and take it back to the plantation center where it would be boiled down in preparation for shipping. These roads made for even better travel.

This was our first real break in almost two months, and we made the most of it, even if we weren't able to go anywhere. On the other side of the coin, other than working on the tracks, there was not much to create any other demands on us. Because we could get unlimited resupply, everyone showered and cleaned up. Perhaps I should explain about living in a track a little more. The inside was about ten feet long by six feet wide and maybe five feet high. Inside this space we stored all of our personal gear, ammo, etc. We were limited to one duffel bag of gear, plus I had a fifty-caliber ammo can for medical supplies, as did many of the men for their own personal gear. These cans sealed out water and just about everything else and made a handy place to keep writing materials, shaving supplies, books, radios, and the like. By the time you had loaded all of the ammo and personal gear, you'd taken up most of the space on the sides and about two feet of the floor. Plus, you had to have the C rations and water.

Water was stored in five-gallon Jerry cans that we placed in the back next to the rear ramp. Because there had to be water for the radiator of the vehicles and we could never be certain of resupply, we had to use it sparingly. Most of the time we didn't get showers more than once a week, and longer was not unusual. The shower consisted of wetting yourself down with a can of water resting on the side of the ACAV, soaping yourself up, and then rinsing off. With a little care, two guys could wash up in five gallons of water. Four guys lived in that space. One was reluctant, for very sound and obvious reasons, to sleep on the ground unless it was necessary. In the rainy season, everyone who wasn't on guard crammed themselves inside as best they could. The hatch was covered with a poncho, and you slept as best you could. There was an obvious aroma to the area with everyone's moldy, damp clothes and bodies, but it wasn't as bad as you might think because after a short period of time you adapted to it. After all, you smelled like they did. You only noticed it a lot if you showered and everybody else didn't. During the dry season, you could sleep on top with care. This was marginally a little riskier, but the extra sleeping space was worth it. If you added me to the group, it made it even more cramped. The trade-off was that they got an extra person for guard duty. Plus, everyone liked to have the medic with them.

Clothing was always a problem. Because there were no laundry facilities and no sewing repair other than little hand kits, any damage to the clothing put you in a bind. You had only six sets at best, so you rationed the clothing carefully. If it got wet, you kept wearing it; likewise if it was dirty. At best you changed clothes twice a week, often less. The dirty clothes you stuffed in a bag and hoped that maybe you'd get a chance to get them cleaned. Because the clothes took such a beating, often rather than get our own clothes back when we got laundry, we got used clothing that had been turned in by GIs before they went back home. The patches, names, etc. were taken off and then issued to us. It didn't bother us a whit as long as they were clean. We weren't worried about anyone inspecting us out there anyway. Our officers were quite tolerant of how we dressed. They were nattier than we were—they probably also got better supply—but they recognized our problems. Unless we were just dreadful, they didn't say much. We frequently didn't shave, but as long as it wasn't too bad, there wasn't any grief. Obviously, there weren't any electric razors out there. Nobody polished boots. Besides the inherent problems of keeping them clean, to say nothing about keeping them dry during the rainy season, nobody wanted to have gleaming boots that would reflect anything anyway. We all wore slouch hats instead of baseball caps. While the baseball caps were official issue, the slouch hats took more abuse, kept rain off of all sides of the face, could be rolled up, and made you look like a combat veteran instead of some camp jockey. After a few weeks of boony-humping, we tended to take a dim view of the regulations and foofaraw of the base camp turkeys.

No one wore underwear out there. Besides being very hot and sweaty and giving you crotch rot, the GI briefs were hopeless. They didn't have jockey shorts, and the briefs were very baggy and had the distressing characteristic of never staying closed. This left the not infrequent occurrence of having the family jewels hung up on the underwear. Plus, the underwear in that humid climate rolled up on the legs and chafed the groin badly. This could be a real problem in that hot, sticky climate. Crotch rot could get so bad that it could get infected and actually incapacitate you. Junior was the driver of the vehicle that I spent a lot of time on, and he got a really bad case of the rot. The driver sat up front on the left of the track, right next to the motor. This got really hot, and he sweated a lot up there. He got a case of the rot that extended from the groin down to below his knees. It was so bad that we had him stand up on the vehicle at every break, drop his pants, and fan himself dry before re-powdering himself. This, of course, left him open, pun intended, to a variety of humorous lines as to his anatomy, physical condition, and prognosis, to say nothing as to how he got it.

Because we had unlimited water at An Loc, everyone showered at once and got clean clothes. We hadn't been there very long before the local Vietnamese learned that we were there and rode their motor scooters out to sell us sodas, beer, and what have you. We obviously worked on the vehicles but generally took it easy and got caught up on our mail, repairing clothes, even looking at newspapers. We couldn't do much of that out in the boonies because we were always on the move.

The next day they told everybody that there was going to be a formation called, and we had to get all spruced up, as much as was possible. Everyone had to be shaved; even the boots had to be polished.

Colonel Patton flew in and passed out medals to some of the GIs, and to my utter surprise, I was one of them. They had impacted the awards, meaning they had made some instant decisions on the award recommendations and then cut some paperwork in order to give the award before everything had been typed up. I hadn't even known that anyone had put my name in. A couple of our guys got Silver Stars and they gave me a Bronze Star and a Purple Heart. I'm not certain which surprised me more. I certainly didn't expect a Purple Heart for my burn. I had only turned it in to protect myself if it got badly infected in the jungle and the docs would know when it all started. Likewise, I didn't feel that I had done anything to deserve a medal. I told my sergeant that, but he kind of put me down and told me to give it back if I didn't want it. The citation they read only sounded a little like what I had done. The awards were certified through the commanding general of the 1st Division as we weren't authorized to give out awards and we were operating under their direction at the time. We waited and waited and never got any documentation. Finally, about four months later, they discovered that the papers had been lost, and consequently new papers were sent in, but they had to guess on the citations because too many people had moved on. But the new awards were complete, and the awards were made official. For if they gave you the award but you never had the orders cut to make it official, it hadn't really happened, no matter what you said. The new citation bore only the vaguest resemblance to what I really did, although it did have the date right. But as we used to say at the time, that and a buck would get you a cup of coffee. Certainly, back in the world (or "real world," as home was called) nobody cared what you had. You were all baby killers anyway.

Awards were kind of funny things in Nam anyway. Certainly they were capriciously awarded. Because there are about five times too many officers in the service in the first place, one would do most anything to get an award as it made you more valuable in the search for promotion. Many an officer went to Nam in the first place because he had to in order to get his "ticket punched." No ticket, no promotions. Many of them were only required to serve six months in the field in the first place. This was very variable depending on the unit you were with. It was probably true that the good units that took pride in what they did and accomplished a lot were the toughest to give out awards. The junk units were far more liberal. It was also true that the higher up you went in the ranks, the more likely it was that you would be over-awarded. One of our squadron commanders got a Silver Star because while flying (read, observing, as he wasn't a pilot) in a small command helicopter, they spotted some NVA on a trail. Valiantly following these enemy soldiers, they pursued them and eventually killed some of them, as if it took any special valor to follow them. I don't think that the pilot got anything, which wouldn't surprise any enlisted GI. Captain West in September got a Silver Star for making himself a target. Lifers were also over-awarded but not as much as officers. If you were under the rank of E6, you probably earned your decoration. Again, nothing was universally true, and I impugn no specific award, but the Top Sergeant who got a Purple Heart because he hit his head on the corrugated metal of the bunker while diving into the bunker in a mortar attack deserved his a heck of a lot less than the guy out working for it. Many of our guys would try and get me to put in papers for an assortment of cuts and bruises, and sometimes I did, but I did my best to describe exactly what it was. I'd let the rear guard dumbos decide what was what. I might stretch things for a guy a little, but I wouldn't lie for him, and certainly not for a Purple Heart.

I'm enclosing a copy of my citation, for what it's worth, and it's not much except that they did give me the medal and my men thought enough of me to put it in.

"Specialist Four Beaven distinguished himself by heroism in connection with ground operations against a hostile force on 29 April,

1969 while serving as a medic with Troop C, 1st Squadron, 11th Armored Cavalry Regiment, in the Republic of Viet-Nam. On this date while conducting a reconnaissance operation, the troop suddenly came under intense small arms, automatic weapons and rocket-propelled grenade fire from a well-fortified enemy force. In the early moments of the firefight, several friendly troops were wounded. Disregarding the hostile fusillade, Specialist Beaven moved into the contact area to administer aid to the casualties. He then moved a number of the wounded to an armored personnel carrier and evacuated them to a secure landing zone. During the fierce battle he made several more trips into the contact area and evacuated a total of fourteen wounded troops to safety and medical assistance. Specialist Four Beaven's courage, devotion to duty and concern for the welfare of his fellow soldiers were in keeping with the highest traditions of the military service and reflect great credit upon himself, his unit and the United States Army."

✝

FAMILY LETTER - 05.1969

For today's essay I'll attempt to describe some of the reactions to the war among the GI's I know. First of all, let me destroy the fallacy that the army makes men. Rubbish! The only thing the army made anyone was resentful. However, like anything else, you can get back exactly what you put in, with dividends. But when they get over here, everyone's just like they were at home. They're just a little more blatant.

A lot of men I know here have grown up quite a bit by stateside standards. They're a lot more responsible, although they'd never admit it. They're neater, usually, and that's also taboo. They've learned to respect people as equals and to live with them, even though they don't like them. Yet they don't discern any of this. When they reach Nam all of this stays with them but it's secondary. The basic emotions of fear, love, hate, desire, etc. are much more vital. Obviously, everyone feels that it's "eat, drink, and be merry for tomorrow we die." Without admitting that they'll ever be dead.

They're also in a place where they feel like they can have anything they want, so they do. Yet, even here the average man feels he has to maintain his status. This status is that of being a man. What is a man here? He's cool in combat, holds his liquor, has plenty of women, laughs at death, or rather refuses to recognize it, and gets along with the guys. Sounds a lot like back home doesn't it?

But it's more than that and it's hard to describe. It's doing your share and protecting your buddies. It's being able to laugh. It's having a girl back home. It's combat. You can't describe the war man because it's the combination of everyone you're around. War is the great equalizer. No matter how big a fink you may have been, it's how you react when the shooting starts that counts. People can be very tolerant because their lives may depend on it. The non-smoker, non-drinker, non-womanizer, non-weapon carrier, non-everything is accepted for who he is until he shows that he's not to be trusted with the lives of his buddies at stake. Then, he can hang it up, like anyone else.

Obviously with the basic emotions so vital they've discovered a myriad of ways to cover them up. Being dumb westerners who consider the showing of emotions as evil, every man develops his own defenses. The favorite is laughter. A real man is very popular because people relax and hide. Very close behind it is sex. Here, where sex is cheap, accepted, and often encouraged, it's a natural to hide behind. The GI is naturally coarse around women and over here, why not? Commanders expect it and don't play "God" because they know it helps tensions. Whereas the other way only makes for cheating and skulduggery. Sex is cheap, 3 or 4 dollars often, and plentiful. It's expected that when someone gets a pass he'll indulge, simply because everyone else would. And to be brutally realistic, it's effective and anyone who says otherwise is naive, without combat experience, and wildly rigid by combat norms. Of course it makes all the girlie magazines popular. Pictures are plastered everywhere, and it's great to talk about and laugh at.

After sex is booze, another basic treatment. Stateside beer is cheap and drinking is common. It's the great palliative. Then, of course, there's the emotional defenses. It's impossible to withdraw so they go to the other extreme and brag. Few are blatant because the braggart is usually disliked and not trusted. They do talk a lot about home, what they've done, what they'll do, etc. And they take a great deal of pride in it all. State pride is common. No one says anything about it, they just put in their two cents worth when the other guy runs down.

Tobacco is not a defense here at all. Nor are families mentioned with regularity. Close girl friends and wives aren't talked about in bull sessions, they are protected and special. Girl friends in general and past lovers are regular fare however. The world situation means nothing unless it's near home. Politics are scorned. The GI is a cynic. He expects nothing, lives for the present and the Freedom Bird back to the world. Yet through it all there's something left to be said for him. No matter how negative one is about him or how bad he seems. No matter what he says, does, or has done. No matter how cynical, disrespectful, or crude he acts. There is still one thing more.

In every GI, from somewhere, there is a seed of, and I hate to use the word, "purity." He acts so gruff but melts eventually. He kicks kids away, but usually ends up smiling. He's so worldly, but give him a chance and he can get a big kick out of the simple things. Most GI's are like Americans at home, little kids at heart. Give them a chance to relax, to trust some one without worrying whether he'll get shot, to let down his hair, and he'll be like everyone else. If America will let him forget the horror, make him honorable instead of despised, shake his hand instead of throw a stare, and use the good that knowledge can bring, then we'll have something.

It can be so funny it scares me. I'm proud I'm here, I'm not going to like to defend it at home. Nor will the others. The GI doesn't recognize any of this and doesn't want to. Why should he? What good is life if you have to think about it? Living it is hard enough. Someone will have to wake up the world again at home. The GI does not like being away from his Laodicean world of unconcern. He grasps at understanding his reactions, understanding in part and trying to fit the puzzle of why. Why he's here? Why men die? And why he is as he is?

He finally knows why he's here and he no longer fights back at it all as he did. He doesn't like it, but it's accepted. He places the ultimate of himself with those he waits for at home. Without saying it he says it all. Maybe it's spread around in a big jigsaw puzzle, but the burden is there. Only so much can be drunk, eaten, laughed or indulged away. The reason for it all is back at the person on the other end. I just hope Americans use the common sense they claim they have, vote to give, pay to see, and never hear. Maybe they'll learn it won't come in a speech. Only from home.

✝

CHAPTER 10

We headed back into the jungle west of the main road and began boony-humping again. Things generally moved pretty slowly, as it did most days, but there were occasional moments of suspense. We had one episode where we were moving through some light forest at a moderate clip when someone looked down and discovered that half of the troop had driven over a 250-pound bomb that was embedded in the ground. This made everyone feel really bright, and we blew it up with C4 after we bypassed around it. We found several bunker complexes, but without anyone who wanted to dispute our right to be there. After trying to destroy them, we'd move on to another spot on someone's map.

We had several dismounted patrols during this period. This was where some guys would be delegated to go trooping across the jungle to some particular spot and set up ambushes. We were a first-class cavalry unit, but their dismounted discipline stank, even for a no-body like me. Because my guys went, I went. We'd sit out there in the rain under our ponchos and hope that nobody came by. The problem would be that the ponchos crackled when you moved, which Charlie could hear, but nobody wanted to take them off and get soaked at night. They preferred to take their chances, and there was no one who could command them to change. Fortunately, we were in luck that night. Some of our guys would use their flashlights to find things, and some of the certifiable idiots would even smoke, as if Charlie couldn't smell cigarette smoke or see lights. For that matter, if we'd been smart, we'd have gotten wet and bagged the ponchos. You could hear the ran pelting on the ponchos for quite a distance. None of my guys had any contact on a dismount, and I feel no sense of loss to not having to have to patch someone up with the troop a mile away. One of our platoons did catch some NVA walking down a trail, but by the time the sergeant got his tank turned around, they had gone. He should have just used one of their machine guns, as was pointed out to him later, but we tended to learn these things by experience. There certainly weren't any textbooks to float around out there.

On one of these trips across the countryside, we were sent to surround a village that intelligence had told us was full of VC. Why they'd use a noisy unit like the Cav, I'll never know, but we did it just before sundown, and we all nervously waited for the troops to go in the next day and clean them out. We were feeling pretty cutthroat right about then, as well as pretty tired, and I don't think we'd have tolerated too much if they'd had started firing at us. I can appreciate what happened at My Lai, whether or not I agree with what they did. But the stress of constant tension with worry about contact, not enough sleep, seeing your friends blown away, etc. lowers your tolerance level considerably. It is certainly true that none of us believed that any "gook" village was worthy of one of our guys. I still believe it, but not because they were "gooks." As a Christian, I believe that their lives are intrinsically as valuable as mine. As an American, I felt my buddy was worth my risking my life for him, and dying for him if necessary. But my life wasn't worth playing any games with the possible chance that the enemy played by the same rules of fair play when there was ample evidence that he'd use any rules he wanted, when he wanted.

My memory's fading a little, and I can't remember the exact time frame but there was one quick trip back to Blackhorse to get some sort of supplies. While there I got to see a Zippo in action. This was a modified track that basically carried a large gasoline tank in the back and that fired napalm. They were using it to burn off the brush that was encroaching on the camp. Theoretically, the Zippo was to be used for bunker complexes but, as can be imagined, it was nothing more than a motorized bomb and wasn't used much. Then again, you wouldn't have hurt very long if it had gone off.

We also spent some time with some infantry riding with us. They enjoyed riding as opposed to foot slogging, and I didn't blame them a bit, but they didn't have much of any idea what combat was like in the Cav. In July we ran into some action at another bunker complex while the infantry was with us. Some tried to hide inside the vehicles, and we had to literally throw some of them out. Others tried to hide behind the vehicles, a thoroughly perilous position. We came within six inches of running over one GIs foot because he was too scared to move and we couldn't get the driver's attention. In combat, he yanked his seat adjustment to drop down low and put his head out of the way. He then looked through periscopes at the outside; plus, he had his radio helmet on for communication with the track commander; plus there was the noise and confusion of combat. All of which made it difficult to communicate. Some of the movies aren't too bad as far as visualizing combat, but they can't capture the 360-degree surround sound and video of chaos, nor the surge of adrenalin with heart pounding, fear gripping your insides, and paralysis of your mind. Many of the foot GIs would lie on their backs in some kind of depression or cover and then hold their M16s pointing backward over their heads and fire that way so as to not expose themselves. Of course, the likelihood of their hitting anything was equally as low. Certainly, the infantry had a better respect for us after that. They didn't like the idea of being on a big target in the middle of a fight, to say nothing about sitting up or even standing during the fight.

On July 6, the troop hit a bunker complex, and we had another major fight. The troop, of course, went into its well-oiled routine, and we went right at them. Several vehicles were hit with RPGs, and there were some wounded, but it didn't seem as intense as the first fight. I probably just had more experience by then. Once everyone had to duck as fighters came and dropped napalm.

Married GI's had a good chance of going on R&R to Hawaii and meeting their wives. Here, the wives are lined up waiting for the husbands to get in from the airport.

Sadly, someone got hurt and died. It took just a long time, including a break for resupply. This was one of the few times that I was wondering about my stand about carrying a weapon. I had moved some wounded back to the rear, which happened to be several hundred yards back along the typical track of mashed-down bamboo, trees, etc. There was a moderate-size bunker complex there, and as I was walking back, alone, I kept wondering what I would do if Charlie had popped out of one of the bunkers, as he easily could have, and started shooting at me. Obviously I wouldn't have stood there and said, "Nyah, nyah, you can't hit me." And I probably would have missed if I had been armed, but I was a little insecure right then.

Two years later I discovered that I had received an Army Commendation Medal with "V" Device (for valor) for that fight. The citation stretched things a bit. It read, "Specialist Four Beaven distinguished himself by heroism in connection with military operations against a hostile force in 6 July, 1969 while serving as a medic with Troop C, 1st Squadron, 11th Armored Cavalry Regiment, in the Republic of Viet Nam. On this date Troop C was reinforcing Troop A during a reconnaissance when they were suddenly engaged by an unknown-size North Vietnamese Army force using automatic weapons and rocket-propelled grenades. In the initial volleys of intense hostile fire, several vehicles were set aflame and many individuals were seriously wounded. Specialist Beaven, with complete disregard for his own safety, dashed through the hostile fusillade to one of the vehicles' driver compartment. Moving quickly and calmly, he extracted the wounded driver and carried him to a safer position, He then returned to the scene of the fierce firefight and continued to help the injured troopers throughout the area for the remainder of the battle. Through his courage and determination he saved one soldier's life and prevented further injury to many other men. Specialist Four Beaven's courageous actions and concern for the welfare of his fellow soldiers were in keeping with the highest traditions of the military service, and reflect great credit upon himself, his unit, and the United States Army."

I need to explain a bit about awards. If you look at a man's chest for his decorations, the lower decorations are for where you served and how well you served. The decorations on the very top are probably for valor. With the exception of a heavy-ego person, most people don't get into pride about their decoration. Awards were created by the soldiers' officers based on what they had seen of or knew of their actions. This would have to approved by the higher-ups. An award such as the Congressional Medal of Honor requires multiple witnesses and an investigation to verify his deeds. If they think that the request is weak or bogus, they may downgrade the award or just throw it away. Many valiant men who would deserve a MOH wouldn't get it because there was no witness to his action. Likewise, there were many valiant men who never got an award simply because they weren't in a position of that kind of danger. A wise man from the SEALs once said that you don't earn awards. They are given to you and you wear them to demonstrate that the military will never forget the service and valor of all those who served, were wounded, or died. I have never once felt that I was courageous or merited an award. Many others feel the same way. I was just doing my job. About the best that can be said is that my officers and men must have liked me because they put me in for it. I don't think I did anything special, though.

After the fight we ran around for a while and then went to Lai Khe, a large fortified town and base for the Big Red One about halfway between An Loc and Cambodia. We began repairing vehicles and sprucing up again. I tried to dig some shrapnel out of a lieutenant as he was going on R&R and didn't want his wife to be worried, but I was only partially successful. (Thirty years later, I found that he got a doctor at Saigon who got out the rest before he went to Hawaii.) While we were in camp, we got to go to some of the clubs.

Usually these sold a variety of alcoholic beverages for moderately out-rageous prices and had girls who'd come by and sit on your lap and be friends, etc. They'd ask you to buy the drinks so that they could stay and keep you company. Of course, you'd pay for whiskey and they'd get tea instead, but it was all part of the game. They'd speak fractured English, and often there was a band and a moderate strip tease maybe, but nothing like what you could get in Saigon. After all, this was on base.

I can't remember where exactly, but at one of the bases, and I think that it was Lai Khe, they closed off the PX from us, say-ing that they didn't have enough for all of us. Of course they had hundreds of cases in storage. It was great fun that they got rocketed two days later, and it just happened to land on the PX. It served them right. We did get some beer before they shut us out, and most everyone got good and smashed, based on the theory, of course, that they'd just sweat it off. It was all nonsense, but nobody really cared. There were a few people who got high on marijuana there—at least, I remember smelling the smoke—but there couldn't have been too many doing it. Maybe they were popping pills, but they weren't smoking. I got a chance to stock up on vitamins and other medicines, penicillin, etc. while I was there, which helped as I was getting pretty low. They wouldn't give me what I wanted, but I could scrounge some.

About a week later, my orders for R&R came through. I hopped a chopper to Saigon and the R&R processing battalion. It took a day to process papers, and then we hopped a bird back to Honolulu with a stop in Guam where we could see the B52s that bombed the boonies for us on the airstrip. Most of the GIs were a mixture of excited and semi-beat, at least the combat vets were. We were all spruced up, although I kept the mustache that I'd been growing. My elder brother had sent me some wax and mustache scissors, that I still use, by the way, and I had a fair handlebar mustache by then. I met my wife at the army post on Waikiki, and we took off. We stayed in a hotel that night and went over to a house on the other side of the island that she'd rented through contact with our church's headquarters. We spent the time touring the sights, the Bishop Museum, Sea World, the Polynesian Village, some of the beaches, etc. It was a grand week (five days and six nights, to be specific). I knew that she disliked the mustache, so I shaved it off, but I grew it back again after I got back to Nam, and I've kept it ever since in one form or another, but I never had another handlebar mustache. Reluctantly, I reported back, and we took off back to Nam, with no hurrahs, I can assure you. One of the stewardesses asked the question, "How come you guys are more tired going back than when you came? You're supposed to be relaxing!" The answer was simple. We were cramming every life activity in that we could. The only thing that I took back was a very nice combat knife, complete with whetstone. I had discovered that scissors had a way of disappearing or falling out in the midst of combat, so I used the knife for cutting shirts, dressings, and the like and never had any other problems.

By the time that I got back, the boys were out in the boonies again, although there had been no action, and I rejoined the troop for more boony-humping. We happened to discover a large cache of weapons on one of our forays, which made everyone really excited. The squadron commander and regimental commander flew in and had pictures taken. Several hundred weapons, all nicely preserved, plus explosives and ammo were discovered. The GIs never saw them again. Theoretically, they were used by the Cav to trade for things we needed like water trailers and the like, which probably did happen some, but we always harbored the suspicion that the officers got their share. We had moved north to a deserted fire base called Thunder 4, on the road north of Lai Khe, which we took over for a few days and got some artillery sighted in while we went back out into the boonies. As I mentioned before, this main road had the jungle cut back over one hundred yards from the road, and there was a series of small temporary firebase sites right next to the road. And this was the fourth one heading south from Cambodia. All it really was was some chewed-up dirt at a specific location that had been used before, but the title sounded nice. I got a nice picture with my Instamatic there. My sister had brought me a Nikon camera, which I paid for, and I was taking pictures again. I made a rule that I'd take no pictures of bodies or blood and gore, and I don't think that I regretted it any. Of course, in combat I refused to carry my camera with me. Besides taking the risk of damaging the camera, I didn't want my men to think that they weren't worth my whole attention.

About this time, there had been a question of the senior medic going to the rear. He had been out for a while, and he was waffling as to what to do. First, he was going to leave; then he was going to stay; then he was going to leave, etc., etc. The problem was that out in the boonies he was the boss with no flak, but his butt was on the line. If he went back in, he'd be pretty safe, but he'd be liable to all of the rear-duty grief. Finally, Dr. Cupps got tired of it all, and he ordered him back, and they made me the senior medic. To do this, my platoon made a special trip back to the headquarters troop, and I grabbed my gear and got off. The new medic hadn't arrived yet, so I loaded my gear on the medic track and about a half an hour after we got there, the third platoon took off again. A quarter of a mile down the road, my ex-track, the one that I'd just left, hit a mine. No one was killed, but several got banged up pretty good. You may say what you want about coincidence, but that was the second time that there was no good sound reason why I wasn't badly hurt, and I tended to give the credit to the good Lord, not to chance.

One of the rules of combat was that you never went out a trail that you went in on. A blind man, and Charlie was neither blind nor stupid, could see the trail that the Cav made through the jungle. If you drove down the road, you were to try and follow the tracks of the vehicle in front of you as perfectly as possible. If he didn't hit anything, you wouldn't either. Going around corners, especially in the wet, clay roads, it took a lot of skill, and it was almost impossible not to slide a little. And the farther you were in line, the worse the road was. In this case, he slid just enough for the left track to hit the mine. Charlie didn't leave much room for error.

On one of our forays, we were back in some bush country running around when, lo and behold, somebody spotted someone, and we captured a VC captain who was lost. He was very lucky that he wasn't blown away, as was mentioned by more than one old-timer who commented as to how lax the Cav was getting. Immediately, the intelligence boys came around on their helicopters trying to get him to spill where his buddies were, without much success. They also got a psy-ops helicopter out there, a helicopter with large speakers mounted on it, so that he could broadcast appeals to his buddies. I don't think anything came of it, and our opinion of intelligence and psy-ops didn't go up any after this episode. It was pretty wet all the time, and getting through some of the small rivers could be quite a chore. The first vehicle would go charging down one side and up the other full bore, hoping to make it. By the time the last guys got there, it could be churned up pretty bad. We had to go down a river a couple of hundred yards once to find a spot low enough for us to get back up the other side. One gully was so bad that they called out a portable folding bridge for us. This was a tank chassis with a large folding bridge on it that opened up as it extended and was then placed over the gully, and we all drove across the bridge, which was slicker than pig snot. It was pretty neat. I don't know how practical it was for real combat, but it was impressive at the time.

We lost one of our vehicles on one of our raids because we were apparently too slow getting going to our objective, and the squadron commander yelled at our captain to get our rears in gear. To catch up, we went out a trail that we went in on, and boom, there goes one track. Our captain, so the story went, was the son of a two-star general in charge of Fort Dix who had been relieved of command twice, but we got him as a last choice. I guess that he was nice enough, but some of his decisions were certainly borderline, like going out how you went in or leaving part of your troop behind while you hustled somewhere else. A few weeks later, I became senior medic and finally made Spec 5, eight months slower than I could have, not that I had any insignia to wear or a uniform worth putting a patch on.

We had one interesting duty where we got called to bail out another armored unit. We were hauled off of our operation and then went off into some light jungle and into another plantation. We came upon a cav unit of the 1ˢᵗ Division that had been beat up pretty good and overrun by the NVA. They had taken fair casualties, and it was there that I learned to really appreciate our Cav. Maybe our officers were a little gung-ho and we carried loads of gear that made traveling uncomfortable, but the other unit's gear was pathetic. They had no gun shields for the machine guns. They only carried 3,000 rounds of ammunition, all told. It was true that there was lots of room inside and it was very comfortable, but their barrels overheated, and they didn't have spares. They used their canteens to cool the barrels and ran out of water. They ran out of ammo, and it's hard to impress the enemy if you can't shoot at him. Apparently they were road jockeys for convoys mostly, and they got in over their heads. Charlie left no room for error. If you did it right, you won; if you were sloppy, the price was high, and they paid for it. We didn't get any contact that trip, but we were feeling insecure. Charlie didn't mess with the Cav much unless he had to. It was a policy to leave calling cards, such as playing cards with the Cav insignia on the back, or a Cav patch, on the dead that we left behind. It's certain that Charlie didn't like it much, but he didn't mess with us much either.

We went heading up the road again, but shortly after this, all of the troops joined together and the whole 1st Squadron moved north in convoy to Loc Ninh, the last town just south of Cambodia.

✝

From: Yahoo Member Services > Black ......35A yahoo
To B.
Subject: Medic
Date: Wed, Dec 17, 2014

First, let me tell you how much I have admired you, being a CO, yet, not using that status to your advantage. I remember you dropping by the Evacuation Hospital in Long Binh, I believe, after I had come out of my first surgery and you finding out that I was there. You stated that the Troop had listed me as missing not knowing where I was. One of the bright spots during my stay at the hospital was that just after my surgery, I was taken to the recovery area and while still in a stupor, I noticed shadowy figures coming down the line and stopping by each individual bunk. I smelled a fragrance that I had not smelled in a long time, perfume. As the figures came closer to my bunk, my vision had cleared so that I was able to recognize the figures as female. When they finally approached my bunk, I was introduced to Judy Ann Ford, 1969 Miss America and six other of the contestants (got a kiss on the cheek from her). Some years later (35 to be exact), I contacted her by E-mail at the school she taught in Illinois. She said that she was so surprised to hear from a soldier and states that her visit to Vietnam in 1969 was a real wake-up call for her. She said that she hadn't realized how important their contribution to the USO tour meant to so many young men. She told me that prior to her visit she was unsure of her feelings about the war, but the trip opened her eyes and gave her a new mission to help bring a little bit of America to Vietnam.

Secondly, what ever happened to our Puerto Rican medic? I need to thank him for the "in field" surgery on my ingrown toenail. To this day, I have had no trouble with toe except for a ridge the length of the toenail (clippers have a hard time negotiating said ridge).

There's more that I would like to share but I feel that your ears can only take just so much bending. Maybe in a later E-mail. God Bless.

SSG, Mario O. (Retired).

Vietnam—1969.

Iraq—2004.

✝

**The North Vietnamese Captain got lost and
intelligence tried for more information.**

CHAPTER 11

Loc Ninh was a lovely little town about ninety miles north of Saigon and seven miles south or east of Cambodia. It was in some small hills south of Cambodia and was the center of a very large series of rubber plantations. It was a great place for the Cav to operate because of the long open rows between the files of trees and the low, rolling hills. It was moderately higher in elevation than the plains and was considerably cooler than farther south. Just to the west of the town was an air strip big enough for small resupply planes. There was a Green Beret base there at the strip, and we stopped there as we were getting into town, so to speak. Some of us got into the camp, and we went down to their entertainment bunker. The bar was very nice, complete with color TV, stereo, etc. They had more soda and beer stashed in their storeroom than we'd seen in over a month, without any exaggeration. And, in fact, they let us buy some from them, bless their hearts. The camp had an A-Team of Green Berets with a company of mercenaries.

The mercenaries had been trained by the Berets and were reasonably disciplined. They were also very gung-ho. They were paid a bounty for every enemy they killed or captured and were thus very aggressive. We went on several operations with them riding on the tracks. Once, in particular, I remember when we spotted a couple of people scooting through the plantations, and those little hustlers hopped off the vehicles and were running faster that we could drive in pursuit. If we got shot at, there was no random firing or running away; they were good soldiers.

I can't say the same for the South Vietnamese Army that we worked with. That's not totally true. We had done an operation with some paratroopers a couple of months before, and they seemed to be pretty good troops. The soldiers we had at Loc Ninh, however, were the pits. Several times we got fired at, and they would hide in the bottom of the track, and we'd have to throw them out, literally. Once it happened that there was one in our track who wouldn't get out, and my actions impressed on the rest of the crew that if he hadn't jumped out really fast, the look on my face was such that he'd have ended up on his head if he'd been any slower. You should appreciate how much you relied on each other in the unit. These were my men, and I would die for them if need be, and they'd protect me as well. There are horror stories of POWs being taken up in the helicopters and then being thrown out alive if they didn't talk. I can't condone murder very easily, but I certainly understand their motivation. There wasn't a VC, NVA, or South Vietnamese who was worth a single wound to my guys. I would of course care for them and assist them, but not if it meant damage to my men. If throwing out a VC prisoner got the other prisoner to talk and it saved the lives of my men, then it was worth throwing him out, or torture, or what have you. I really don't accept that last statement, but I can see how men got that way. At any rate, we had been in minor combat, and I do mean minor, with these ARVN (Army of the Republic of Viet-Nam) troops, and each time they ran away. Worse, one of our guys got some minor wounds because one of their idiots fired an M79 grenade over our heads and down the road, from thirty yards behind us, along the column of vehicles. But we were in a rubber plantation with trees everywhere, and the grenade hit a limb and exploded over our guy's head. They immediately hid the moron, or he might have ended up as dog meat. There was no tolerance at all for people who ran and less than that for those who hurt our guys through stupidity.

The Green Berets out there seemed pretty nice and understood that we were working joes. I can't say the same for many of their buddies. They were trained in basic medicine and surgery at Fort

Sam, and most of those we saw at MTC were really stuck up and better-than-thou. The same was true with the rear-guard types who really strutted around. On one trip to town with some of these guys, we got to go to one of their bases for the Berets at Long Binh, and let me assure you, they lived well. Their bar was at least the equal of any that I've seen here in the States. On the same trip, I got to eat my one and only Vietnamese meal at a restaurant there. It was okay, but me thinks that unless you knew what you were doing, there was an acquired taste to it. The ARVN soldiers almost always ate just plain rice, and rice seemed to be in most of the dishes at any rate, and that got old really quick. Other than when I was at the mission, that was my only non-GI meal during my whole tour, and it was a treat no matter what the food was made of. Some of the air force bars and accommodations were pretty spiffy as well. It was rare for any of our guys to be unhappy with the boys in the rear; we just envied them their goodies, and we worked for our chance at jobs in the rear. We congratulated the joe who got one and hoped for our turn. On the opposite side of the coin, we didn't like being sneered at or treated like lepers.

Just as in WWII, as Bill Mauldin so graphically pointed out, or in Korea, or in any war, I'm sure, the guys in the rear tried to milk the glory without having to work for it. They "deserved" any goodies they got, and it was their right and duty to preserve it. Whereas the guy who was humping and rarely got any goodies got dumped on. It was our unit that pulled guard duty for Bob Hope and the USA show. We got the Korean dancing girls. We got the PXs that would shut down and not serve us. We got harassed by officers because we didn't look or smell pretty, as if there was anything we could do about it. Bars wouldn't let us in. Unclean! Once, one of the bars in the rear base camp, theoretically a combat unit, wouldn't let our boys in for beer. After six weeks in the boonies, our guys just wouldn't stand for it. They weren't allowed anywhere else, and where they could go wouldn't let them in. Sooooo, they got their M48 and pushed open the door with their ninety-millimeter cannon and asked if they could come in after all. It's amazing what courtesy you get when you know the right way to ask.

We got to work with a large variety of troops during the tour. The ARVN generally stank, with the exception of the paratroops. We worked with some Aussies down south once, which was kind of fun. They were fun-loving, irreverent guys who weren't into harrassment much. We didn't have any contact, so I can't tell you how they fought, but we enjoyed their company. They sure enough did enjoy their beer. The Americans, while never even close to the ARVN, did run the gamut from poor to pretty good. The 1st Air Cav seemed reasonably with it. Some of the rest were just along for the ride. They certainly weren't ready to fight. While we never worked with them, the stories about the Koreans made them to be pretty tough cookies. The ROK (Republic of Korea) troops, perhaps because they were Asian and understood the mentality, didn't tolerate anything. If they were interrogating someone and they didn't talk, they never got a second chance to rue the decision, and inevitably people talked. Apparently, where they built their base camp someone hadn't ordered the mines for around the perimeter. The ROKs just put up the signs, and no one ever found out because Charlie wasn't at all interested in checking to find out.

We had one bad incident while working with some US infantry. One of their GIs shot himself through the hand and into his stomach while cleaning his .45 caliber pistol. No matter how you get taught, sometimes people get lazy. In combat, there's no room for lazy. He didn't check his weapon. We went flying up to help and started an IV, elevated his legs, and so on. A dust-off was called, but it didn't do any good. It was a bit of a bummer all around. You hate to lose anyone, least of all to something unnecessary. Most of the time, however, we worked alone, which was just as well. Because the infantry hadn't worked with armor, it was often a nuisance to work around each other. I'll grant you they were handy for checking our bunkers—we weren't tunnel rats—but it was easier just worrying about ourselves.

We set up the squadron base at the end of the runway about one hundred yards away from the Beret camp and promptly scattered around and began patrolling. For some reason, Charlie didn't like us there, and life became considerably more hectic. I really don't remember which events happened when, except for the final episodes, but this will be close. First, we headed west of Loc Ninh toward the edge of the plantations, which covered what seemed like a hundred square miles. We ran through a fortified village looking for trails and then started toward the north inside the edge of the plantation. Parts of the plantation weren't actively cultivated, perhaps due to lack of employees, and in some of the remoter areas, there was some overgrowth to obscure things. We came to some areas where there were trails leading away from the rubber, but we couldn't get to the other side of some gullies, so we sent out dismounted patrols. Charlie must have really become lackadaisical; certainly he could hear us even if there were trees between us. But we sent a dismount across the gully on a two-tree bridge, and they were walking along lazily when, lo and behold, they stumbled on a mortar crew setting up their mortar. We weren't expecting trouble either, so guys started firing haphazardly. The upshot was that they got away with the mortar, but we did find some blood trails leading off into the bush toward Cambodia. This, needless to say, got our adrenalin flowing, and it took a while to sort everything out and get going again.

About an hour later, there was a similar area with a trail leading off into some overgrown rubber. Another dismount went off into some overgrown rubber. This dismount went off, a little more prepared mentally, and they came on three guys chowing down around the fire and eating American chow. We started firing and killed two of the three. Every time this happened, I'd grab the aid bag and start running down the trail. Anytime there was firing, you assumed that someone was hurt until you knew otherwise, as Charlie usually took the first shot at armor, but again they weren't expecting us, and none of our guys got hurt. They had scads of our sodas, Orange Crush, Cokes, and the like scattered around their camp, all empty, alas. They had more empties there than we had had in the last three weeks. In Nam you could get anything if you had the money. We had been taught early that you left nothing behind. Your bad batteries that you were throwing away had enough of a charge to set off a mine, and so on. Likewise, the black market could get you anything. And I do mean anything. One of our squadron's medics stole a jeep and drove to Saigon for a bash and sold it to pay for the party. We got him back but not the jeep. If you wanted weapons, uniforms, and whatever, they were available for the right price. After these two contacts, we were aware that Charlie was around and planned accordingly. But even so, we'd go days without contact of any kind.

One night I got roused out of a sleep to find that we were almost left behind. We weren't on guard because we were on the medic track, and no one had thought to wake us. Our battery was dead, and it was thoroughly possible that if I hadn't wakened, we could have been left behind in the dark as you certainly didn't show lights in the middle of the night. And we were so tired that all of the engines starting hadn't awakened us. We hurriedly got a jump start and took off back to the airstrip where one of the other troops had been hit and we were going to their support. They had been laagered up between our camp and the Beret camp, and about 2:00 a.m. one of the guys on guard saw some movement, and they got hit by some RPG teams and sappers. Some got right up in between the vehicles where you couldn't depress the guns before they got taken out by small arms. Afterward they found out that the RPG teams had complete maps of the laager. During the afternoon, the ladies and little kids had come out to sell sodas, souvenirs, and what have you, and they paced off the whole camp. The maps had the numbers of the vehicles and even the names of some of the crews. Everyone in the Nam was your enemy until proven otherwise. Needless to say, the gooks (and if you're trying to destroy me, I'm entitled to call you anything I want) were kept at a distance after that. We headed back southwest to our area and roamed around. We spent one night in a triangular-shaped open area near us, and I bought some nice pictures on cloth as souvenirs that I still have, and we headed to the northeast to a different area the next day. I didn't get much in the way of souvenirs while in Nam, mostly for a lack of money. Much of it was going home to the family. I did get a pair of binoculars. I ordered some China and flatware that arrived home three months after I did. I bought one watch to replace mine that stopped a month after I arrived in Nam. And I bought the Nikon, through my sister. Other than those, I didn't get much. The memories I couldn't have purchased, however.

We next roamed around to the north, occasionally coming back to the center of the plantation. We laagered up one time in a low area off to one side of the main plantation and formed a big circle around a deserted building, and it was here that I was taken off of guard duty. A few days later we were back, and that evening we were mortared. We had some ARVN troops as infantry around us, to the outside with our tracks laagered up face out as always. The ARVN often slept in hammocks hung off of the ground by small poles, which proved dangerous that night. One of the sayings in war is that there are the quick and the dead. If you're any good at all, you develop instincts and reactions that you can't measure. After a couple of months, I could recognize the difference between incoming and outgoing. This was important because our general fatigue wouldn't allow us to be awake to cogitate on these things. We had once served as guards for a 155 mm howitzer battery, and they'd have these fire missions in the middle of the night. This huge cannon would go off without warning from twenty feet behind your vehicle. After the first month or two, we slept right through them. A mortar, especially the small pack-carried mortars, has to be fairly close to be able to hit you. When they fire, they have a hollow pop sound from the tube. That night I woke up with the first pop, not remembering or hearing the pop sound and wondering what was happening. I heard the second pop, and I was wide awake when the first explosion went off. Charlie walked the rounds in to the perimeter and dumped at least twenty rounds, or more, on us in pretty quick order. We were sitting in the track with the top open (the hatch had broken off), hoping that the mortar rounds wouldn't come through the hatch, a potentially messy event. Many of the ARVN, who had been sleeping up off of the ground, got hurt in the first rounds before they could get flat. None of our guys got badly hurt, but the ARVN got messed up a bit. We did get one casualty that we didn't miss at all. This was the new shave tail (second lieutenant) who was all vim and vinegar but had a few synapses missing. He was one of these guys who talked a lot but with no experience to back it up. I appreciate enthusiasm as much as the next guy, but when he had all these neat plans and hadn't even bothered to check them out with guys with experience, one became a little skeptical. He took over command of a platoon, which was horrified to hear over the radio net, several days after they had been on patrol, him asking his platoon sergeant how to cock the fifty-caliber in front of him. This was not an episode to instill confidence. He was in the cupola where one of the rounds went off in the mortar attack and which sent some shrapnel into his arm. Early on it didn't bother him, but about fifteen minutes later he was moaning and groaning and really uncomfortable.

As with all units, there was attrition and replacement of the troops. I had several new medics, and one in particular had been left out when they were passing out genes for common sense. After the mortaring stopped and we were sorting out the casualties, he came to me looking for some praise because he had been out crawling around the ARVN trying to help. I'm afraid that I disillusioned him a bit, even though I appreciated his courage. In the first place, he knew no Vietnamese and could neither talk nor diagnose in the dark. Next, he used a flashlight to diagnose injuries, which was borderline insane. If I were wounded, I sure would hope that he'd help someone else. Lights make great targets. Next, the ARVN had their own medics; he left his boys to go a-wandering. Next, he exposed himself needlessly. Mortar attacks didn't last long, and unless we were going to be attacked by ground troops, you should just wait and then handle the casualties when you could be organized. By the way, he didn't find any wounded that needed his help. He meant well, but he needed to take care of his men.

We loaded up our wounded and took off for the landing strip, going down the road with just three vehicles, each short a gunner, in the dark and driving without lights. It was misty and foggy at the top of the hill, and the chopper came in about 4:30 am but couldn't see us. We could see him and his light, and we were in radio contact, but he couldn't see us. Unfortunately, he wouldn't trust us to talk him down, and there was nothing within a hundred yards. I can't speak for his rules of flying, but we were really angry that our wounded had to wait four hours for a plane to come in and take them away. We had always had good support from the helicopters. To be fair, they had never been in any major risk when with us as we could always create a safe zone farther back from the action, but they always came when we needed them. To be left in the lurch like this when we could see them less than fifty feet over us was remarkably irritating.

We headed off east of Loc Ninh for a while working with both the mercenaries, and later the ARVN. We had several light contacts, once when we saw three people scooting through the trees, and chased them. They turned out to be just local people, although I'll bet you they were VC, no matter what their papers said. I'm sure that we scared people, but when you run away, you sure do make people suspicious. We had an episode with the ARVN where they fired that

M79 launcher over our heads from a ways behind us. We had seen some people moving through the trees from a distance and started after them. The ARVN jumped off and ran the other way when the shooting started. We spread out some and continued shooting. We were just at the edge of the rubber, and they disappeared into the bush on the other side, but we didn't pursue into it and the ARVN wouldn't chase them. Our mezzo-bright medic jumped off his tank when the shooting started but dropped his aid bag into the bottom of the tank and forgot where he left it. He came up to me later, looking for it. He didn't impress his platoon much by losing his aid bag. A little later we found some NVA running through the trees, and we got the jump on them. We've got a lot of fire power, and you should either run or be prepared. They tried to do both. They'd hide behind a tree and then scoot quickly to another and then another, trying to avoid the bullets. But we had more than one vehicle, so you could only do it so long. Worse, they'd stop to shoot at us. Whereas our fifties could chew a small tree in half, if need be. Only one got away from that crowd.

A few days later they had us back up at the air strip to do some maintenance. We were laagered up between our camp and the Berets, where the other troop had been hit a couple of weeks before. The place was an absolute mud hole—it was still rainy season—and there were a few places so deep that you could literally, without exaggeration, lose a track in the mud up to the cupola. It was hard keeping dry, and in fact you couldn't really be totally dry. The tracks were musty and muddy. Clothes stayed damp because we were living out of sacks and closed-up spaces. I got a chance to mosey down to the squadron medics and chitchat a little and pick up a little news. I almost never heard anything about what was happening to the other medics or units. We just kept slogging away at our jobs. We had a Spec 6 medic with the unit then. He was an LPN and basically ran the medics. Dr. Cupps was in charge, but the scut was run by him. He had this bad hand tremor that would shake constantly up until the moment he had to do something, and then it would smooth away. It was fun watching him suture or cut as he'd have this shaking needle heading for someone's skin but then be totally smooth when the needle touched the skin. One of the evenings that we were laagered up we got a little excitement. They had a mad minute on the perimeter; this was a minute when out of the blue everyone started firing at the tree line to stop anything going out on the edges. Alas, someone sent a round into the ammo dump, which was on the other side of the runway from the camp and a couple of hundred yards away. It was beautiful and a lot like some movies. There'd be whistling sounds of rounds going off, colorful explosions, and so on. It was ten o'clock at night, sudden rattles like a machine gun, and so on. It was hard to keep your head down because you wanted to watch it all, and it lasted for at least ten minutes. It was fine entertainment, and I was glad that I hadn't shot off that round.

Shortly after this, we went back up to the north again. I guess that they were rotating the troops around so that they'd know the area. A few days later, we were in troop column, meaning that I was fourth or fifth in line, just behind the Captain, who was behind two Sheridan tanks and one ACAV, when we got hit by an RPG in the lead tank. It was shot from up ahead on the right about two-thirds of the way up a small hill. They had fired from one of the drainage ditches that they had around the hills. And while the open files of trees made it easy for us to travel around, those ditches made it easy for them to move around and stay under cover. The team must have been lunatics, though, because while they had several launchers and rockets, to have expected to have hit enough of us to stop us from overrunning them was remarkably naive. I happened to see the rocket coming, having turned that direction on hearing the initial whoosh. It was the only time that I can swear that I saw one coming. Of course there was no time to shout a warning. Immediately I hopped off of the medic track, on the away side of course, and ran for the lead vehicle while the rest of the Cav spread out and took off after the RPG teams. The Sheridan had a crew of three men. The loader got knocked off and had some minor injuries. He was on the away side of the round and didn't get hurt. The tank commander was also lucky. He picked up some minor wounds and got knocked inside and beat up a little. He crawled out and was with his loader. He was absolutely irate about getting knocked out of the battle. His driver buttoned up his hatch and was just sitting there. Meanwhile, there were grenades smoking at the top hatch, which made life a little interesting. I beat on the hatch of the driver, but either he couldn't hear me or he wouldn't open up. I was really reluctant to crawl through the hatch with the smoking grenades, for some readily apparent reasons, unless it was absolutely necessary. We didn't know if the driver was wounded or not, and I was getting a little anxious and was on the tank ready to brave it out when he opened his hatch. He had been just sitting there waiting for orders. He was new and didn't have enough sense to bail out of a hit track that was smoking. We didn't lose any other casualties, and there were no other RPG hits. What the teams may not have been aware of was that you just couldn't stand and leisurely aim while thirty or more machine guns were aiming at you. It was a high-risk occupation. You might get the first shot, but if you weren't really prepared, you were in deep doo-doo the moment the first round went off.

To show how combat ready we were, we were laagered up in some brush north of the road running on the edge of the rubber. We had put out our Claymores, grenades, and things that rattled when moved and settled down and set up guards. In the middle of the night, we got an RPG attack, but the rockets went over us. But everyone held their fire as there weren't any targets. The next morning, they checked their Claymores, and every Claymore had been turned around. If our guys had lost their discipline, who knows how many of our own guys would have been killed or injured by our own mines.

NDP OUT SIDE OF LOCK NINH

On Sept. 6, 1969 we set up an NDP out side of Loch Ninh. That night SSG. Bob D. took out an ambush patrol. And about midnight the gooks attempted to sneak in on us and Bob and his patrol sent them home early. Of course when Bob and his guys opened up on them so did the rest of the troop.

The next morning we were sent out on a search and destroy mission. I was an E-R Sheridan T.C. so being the lowest rank T.C. we got to lead. We were told to go out the road that we had made coming in and when my driver, Gary S. and I questioned that we were told "use the road" but watch out for mines. Just as I reached for the switch on my C.V.C. to tell SFC. B not to worry, if there were any out there we would find them, we did. I can still hear him screaming at SSG. D to find out what happened. Bob told him #29 just found the mines. Well, as usual Doc B was there before the sound of the blast quit echoing. Gary received minor injuries as did I, but we still had to attempt to fix 29 as best we could. When we got finished 1st Sgt C told us that we would probably be overrun that night and that we were to get ready. Well, as things went Gary was sent Saigon due to his injuries. I left to go on R&R

to Australia and 1st Sgt C and the few guys that he had left weren't overrun. I would like to thank Gary publicly for being the best driver I had the entire time I was in the military, and Doc B for being there as quick as he was to help us.

Danny W.

Clarksburg, W.Va.

✝

CHAPTER 12

Things quieted down for a few days as we rummaged around north of the plantation. They had us out in small nighttime laagers to try and trap some of the NVA, who were all over the area, even though we hadn't seen them. We made one camp several hundred yards into the bush north of the plantation and only a couple of miles from Cambodia. We could even see into the Cambodian countryside from the hills. We went back out next on the same trail we went in on, but two days later, we came back and camped on the same site. We got hit that night by an RPG team, but apparently they were spotted just before they started firing, and everyone opened up. All of the rounds went high, and neither we nor they took any casualties. It did mess up the night, though. First thing in the morning we got a rush order to get moving to help another troop. We saddled up in a hurry and our idiot captain, in a hurry to get to our post, took us out the same trail, and sure enough, the lead track hit a mine. We went flying up the trail to help the casualties, but no one was badly hurt, just shaken. The captain left a couple of tracks to help and the rest of us took off at full bore down the plantation road, heading west. About ten miles away, we came upon A Troop, who'd been hit that morning by some RPG teams. We waited next to their troop, which was scattered a little, while our captain went over to the other troop to confer. While he was gone, we saw some movement in some of the drainage ditches, and some of our vehicles headed down the slope toward the movement.

Boom!! went the first RPG, and the next half an hour became chaos. We had found several RPG teams, and we all went looking for each other. With the first boom, I grabbed my aid bag and went running to help. The first round hadn't hurt anybody, but Charlie wasn't running, and the fighting continued. You could see NVA crawling up ditches. One of our sergeants drove downhill in his Sheridan. We had some wounded from shrapnel that we started patching up, and I went downhill looking for more casualties. Walking down the hill, I stepped over a left hand just lying there. Apparently an NVA had been hit and his RPG rounds blew up, leaving just the hand. Nobody ever saw anything else. We had a KIA (killed in action), unfortunately. One of the tank loaders looked out of his hatch as the tank drove by someone who popped up out of his drainage ditch. He was shot in the left temple and there was nothing that we could do. Eventually we either killed or chased away everyone, and we were left with one KIA and several wounded. They elected to send the medic track, with two escorts, back to the landing strip for a dust-off.

We loaded up the wounded and took off. You should understand that we were shorthanded. Because of casualties, R&Rs, and the like, the three tracks had one driver, one gunner, and the commander in the lead track. Our track had the driver and commander and me, but I wouldn't use the machine gun. The third track was also a man short. This did nothing to increase our confidence. We knew that Charlie was all over everywhere, so we went moving as fast as our tracks could hustle, somewhere around forty-five miles per hour. We went flying around the corners of those dirt roads. We passed some ARVN on patrol, but we trusted them not a whole lot more than we trusted Charlie. It was a good ten minutes back to the landing strip where we went first to the squadron aid station. There was a TV crew there filming, but there wasn't much to see. After looking at the casualties, Doc Cupps had us drive them up the strip to a spot where a dust-off came in, and we loaded them up and took off back to our unit.

My track commander was a country boy who worked his way up through the system to his present position. The other two track commanders were instant NCOs. These were guys who went to a special brief course back in the States that taught them to be noncoms, the army being shorthanded, I guess. As could be expected, many of these were full of their own importance, never having been on the receiving end. The sergeant ostensibly in charge of our threesome had had a run-in with me a couple of months before. We weren't enemies, but I doubt that he understood me. I had happened to be riding on his track, and he knew that I wouldn't carry a weapon, but he turned around and told me where I was to put the ammunition he needed if there was a fight, I told him that I wasn't going to hand him his ammunition.

Why not?

Me: Because I wasn't going to help him kill anyone.

But I wouldn't be doing the shooting.

Me: That's immaterial. I was there to save lives, not take them.

I had jolly well better do it or there would be trouble.

Me: What difference did it make? If I hadn't been on the track, he would have gotten his own anyway, right?

Because he wanted it and he was the commander.

Alas, while maybe I would have caved in early in my tour—I doubt it—but I certainly couldn't have been intimidated and harassed late in my tour with the Cav. By that time, with two fights plus under my belt, he couldn't back me down then. I knew what I could do and what was expected of me. His men knew it too, and they told the sergeant to calm down. They'd rather have me with them than with someone else. If somebody got hurt, I was an asset. He hadn't needed me before—back off!

At any rate, this sergeant was now in charge, and we went flying down the road back toward where we had been. We came upon some wounded ARVNs on the road, and I stopped us to load them up and take them back to the airstrip. The TCs didn't want me to stop and pick them up, but I couldn't think of a good reason to leave the wounded behind. We dashed back, unloaded, and turned around quickly and headed back toward the rest of our troop. He took us on a slightly different route back. I guess he thought that there was a shortcut to where we had been. But whereas we had been doing forty-five down the road, now we were doing five miles per hour through the trees and feeling more insecure by the minute. Lo and behold, we got to where we were supposed to have been, and no one was there. So he got on the horn and asked were the troop was. And however much our captain will never be remembered for his greatness, he wasn't so dumb as to tell our sergeant over the radio where they were. So they played guessing games and "Please, Sir's" for a while, and finally our sergeant remembered that open triangle area where we had laagered up before, and we headed down there to join up with the troop.

When we got there, we found that we were the last three vehicles in a troop column with C Troop Commander up in front. The normal position for the medic track was right behind the captain, fourth in line. But there was no good way to get there as there were fairly deep drainage ditches on each side of the road, and we were discouraged from driving on the sides of the roads for fear of mines. And we knew better. We sat there for about five minutes wondering what to do when there was more incoming. I initially thought they were rockets as I couldn't hear any tube sounds, but they were probably mortars. We got hit by maybe twenty rounds in fairly quick succession, and we were a little lucky. Charlie missed the road and hit the field about five meters away. But that was close enough. The Cav spread out carefully and started firing away at an enemy that they couldn't see, and I grabbed the aid bag and went running down the road toward the front of the column. I got to Sergeant Sanders first. He was a hefty guy from Arkansas who had been in the Cav before, gone home for a few months, and immediately volunteered to come back. I don't know what his home life was like, but I could understand his wanting to come back. Back home you had spit and polish, harrassment from turkey officers who didn't know what they were doing, and depending on your job, a fair degree of boredom. Combat was always exciting. You feared the danger, but it made you alert and alive. When you got shooting, there was power in that gun. I had to hit one of our guys on the head to get him to quit shooting his machine gun after "Cease fire!" was yelled because he was so into shooting that gun. He was in control and could feel it. We derided people like that a little, but I personally would much rather have been in the field than back in camp. I could have tolerated a break now and then, but to stay back there would have been a drag.

Wayne crawled off his track onto the side of the road, and he was conscious and in pain. All I could find was a little hole, less than half the size of your little fingernail, in the middle of his abdomen. My assistant, Doc L., came up a short while later. He was always a little slower to get going than I was, so I turned Wayne over to him, and I went forward. It was a mess up at the front. The head of the column was just past the edge of that field, and they hit the side of the field. The command track was a mess. The commander of the track had a wound in the back of his head. We put a dressing on it, and he couldn't see, but we calmed him down. I never did hear what happened to him, but I was fearful because that's where the brain center for sight was. The captain was on the right-hand side, and he had a shoulder wound. We put a dressing on him, and he was dusted off as well. It's hard to judge a man who is wounded, and I'd be the last to do it, even for the captain, but his wound wasn't very big, and he seemed incapacitated by it. I'd seen enough people keep functioning with wounds worse than that, but who can say. I trust that he got well, and I hope that he got his ticket punched in Nam and then retired from the army. He was dangerous. His gunner on the left, Larry B., was a mess.

Larry had every medic's horror, a sucking chest wound. This is a hole in the chest that lets air in through the hole. As he breathed, air was sucked into the chest, which caused the lung to collapse. Theoretically, you closed it with plastic and sealed it off—but it wouldn't work. In today's world, we have special equipment and training to fix this condition. In 1969, your average medic just had a dressing with a sterile plastic cover. The plastic wouldn't seal. Hot, sweaty, bloody chests wouldn't let the plastic stick. A big dressing and pressure helped some. We checked his back for other holes but couldn't find any. He kept wanting to get up, and gradually his breathing got worse and worse and he died on us. We were devastated. In the track behind the captain, where I was supposed to be, there was a track with two of our platoon medics. I'm not certain why both of them were there. Rusty, who was a very good medic, and ding-a-ling, our worthless one. Both of them were wounded, Rusty in the back of the head. They initially stayed with the track and were firing at whatever; then they got off, and we patched them up, and they tried to help. There were some other casualties, but those were the worst.

My assistant had come up to help. He wasn't really slow or dumb; he just didn't have enough experience, namely none, which was why he was with me and not in a platoon, and I finally asked him about Wayne, and he said that he'd died, which stunned me, as he had looked fine when I had left him. I guess that that little piece of shrapnel had clipped his aorta and he had bled to death inside. I really felt bad. Wayne was one of the guys who had talked to me about my faith in God and lifestyle a few weeks before. I hadn't pursued talking to him because of the difficulties in finding time but I was assuming we'd get a break and we could spend some time together. That time never came. Don't ever assume that you'll get another chance. Take it when you get it. Flowers at a funeral are a waste; give them while the people are alive to enjoy them.

We finally got everyone dusted off, including my two medics, and the squadron commander came flying in for a postmortem. Eventually we set off down the road and had gone for maybe a half a mile when more incoming went off in the trees just to the side of the road. We immediately faced out and prepared for fighting, and I hopped off and started back to the vehicles where the rounds were. I can remember feeling so tired that I couldn't even duck. "Oh no, here we go again." I just wasn't prepared to handle more—my legs were like lead—but fortunately no one was hurt. The incoming rounds were artillery that someone had asked for, but we were moving and passed right past where the artillery was shooting. Fortunately, we got that straight in a hurry.

This was the third time that there was an incident where there was no good reason why I wasn't seriously hurt or killed. I'm not a believer much in coincidence. Random chance occurs, but these were far too plain to me. The only time in three months when I wasn't directly behind the captain was that day when the sergeant got us lost. And both people who were in the positions where I might have been in position were dusted off. I wish I knew what had happened to them, but I never found out. I do know that God was looking out after me, for reasons that I don't understand fully. But I do believe that God will protect those who love him, and he cared for me way beyond any rules of chance.

We made it back to laager up and clean up. The lieutenant who had taken over asked me to write up citations for the two medics who were hit, which I did, and proceeded to dress them up as best that I could. The next day we spent cleaning up and were ready to go back at it, but just then Ho Chi Minh died. I'm not certain that anyone really knows whether Ho was a patriot, a Communist, a rejected American suitor from WWII, or what have you. But when he died, there was a three-day cease-fire declared that didn't bother us a bit. We kept running patrols, and I can assure you that I was getting anxious as I had less than a week left in country. Every time we went over a hill, I knew that there would be another fight, but there wasn't. At the end of three days, they told me to grab a chopper back to the rear to get ready to leave. I felt really bad about leaving. Of our five medics, two had been dusted off, and one of the ones who was left had trouble tying his shoes (an exaggeration, because he was new). I didn't want to leave my guys in the lurch with no one who knew anything about being a combat medic. From personal experience, it took time to know what to do. I decided to try and extend my tour, but to do that I had to go the rear anyway. So, I packed my gear and stood by the side of the road in tears as my guys went off without me. I then flew to Bien Hua, where we had a temporary rear camp.

No one in the rear could answer my questions, so I went looking at Long Binh for someone to help, but I was stymied. The army regulations wouldn't allow you to extend unless you had enlisted. If you were drafted, you couldn't be kept over two years against your will. You could voluntarily sign up, but noncombatants weren't allowed to enlist. Thus, even though I was a combat-proven, decorated medic, they wouldn't allow me to stay. It didn't make any sense, but then there were a variety of things about the army that never made any sense.

They put in an award for me, another Bronze Star with V Device, which read, "Specialist Five Beaven distinguished himself by heroism in connection with military operations against a hostile force on 6 September, 1969, while serving as a medic with Troop C, 1st Squadron, 11the Armored Cavalry Regiment, in the Republic of Vietnam. On this date Troop C was in heavy contact with an estimated battalion of North Vietnamese Army soldiers. A rocket-propelled grenade slammed into one vehicle, seriously wounding the entire crew. Specialist Beaven dashed through the hostile fire to aid the injured troopers. He administered aid and then directed their evacuation. Specialist Five Beaven's actions were in keeping with the highest traditions of the military service and reflect great credit upon himself, his unit, and the United States Army."

I got sent to the replacement battalion where, under dire threats, we turned in any NVA leaflets we had as well as clothing, and then we were shipped to Bien Hua to catch the Freedom Bird. With great jeering, just as when we arrived, we harassed the newbies who had just arrived, and we hopped on board Flying Tiger Airlines for the flight back. After last-minute jitters, fearing mortars as we took off or some such, we flew north to Japan. There was initial cheering as we left the ground, but then everyone pretty much settled down, probably in reaction to finally going home. In Japan we saw nothing as the whole country was covered over with clouds, and we landed at an air force base. We were allowed only in the air base building while they cleaned and refueled, so we saw nothing. At 3:00 a.m. we arrived in Anchorage, Alaska, and got to wander around an empty airport terminal, and again saw nothing. That afternoon we landed to great cheers at an air base in New Jersey. They bussed us to Fort Dix for out processing. We were given a new uniform and final pay. I then grabbed a bus to the airport, and my tour with Uncle Sugar was done.

In retrospect, it was a good thing for me to go to combat. It was an awful way to learn confidence and success. To this day, I pay the price of my childhood. But those years were the first time that I could say totally I did my job. I made a couple of mistakes but not many. My guys wanted me. I had succeeded. When I got back to college, some of the macho guys who had pushed me around, couldn't. I might have backed off because I didn't like confrontation, but it wasn't because I had to—it was because I chose to. Not a single drop of blood was worth that knowledge, and the good Lord had to intervene for me to learn it, but having survived intact, I can praise him for this knowledge and wisdom.

✝

Doc,

I very seldom get serious on the subject of Vietnam, however I will for a little bit now. I just say that I met, became friends with, and surprisingly am still good friends with some of the guys I met over there. We grew closer, probably out of necessity, than some families do unfortunately. We may, like you said, have had our difference of opinions over the war, how it was handled, and in some cases religion or religious beliefs and the war. There were a few times I know of when you, your beliefs and the war bothered some people, however, in the end everyone had high regards for you because when the chips were down, so to speak, you more than some others, always did your job with the highest honor and integrity. A few occasions I can remember is when you were on guard outside of Loch Ninh and didn't shoot the gooks that passed and you were the only one to see them. There were some who had hard feelings for a while, however, I know that one time after a fire fight you were checking to see how everyone was and I asked you, "Doc what are you going to do one of these days when you bail off a track in the middle of a fire fight and go running to where one of the guys are injured and to your surprise a gook jumps up in front of you with an AK-47, what are you going to do?" and you answered, "I will give him my ID card, tell him I don't have time right now, find me later, and keep on running to help." I liked you before that incident, but I did not have much respect for you because I did not understand your feelings and beliefs. I was a Preachers son, and I still did not understand, however after that short conversation a whole bunch of respect jumped all over me for you because you had your beliefs and had the courage to stick with them. I will also say that you made it hard on the medic that replaced you, because we all compared him and you and told him that he had a long way to go to even get to tie your boots. He, unlike you though, was a very good shot with an M-16, and perhaps he should have been infantry, because I saw him plunk off gooks at long distances with an M-16, and he was like us. But he never had the respect that you earned and gained. I also know how to this day some feel about you, one person told me that if it weren't for you, he would definitely be dead, another guy also says that you saved his life and he will never forget it. And personally, Doc, I remember September 7, 1969 outside of Lock Ninh, a young smart ass named Weas..... was the TC of a lead Sheridan leaving our night defensive position. This TC was told that the road may be mined and before I got the chance to answer, and I do remember exactly what I was going to say, just as if it was yesterday, there was a very loud explosion, everything went into slow motion instantly and I was thrown all over the TC hatch. Before the sound of the explosion was gone I looked down to my right and you were there wanting to know if I or anyone on 29 were injured. You saw the blood running down my arm and wanted to take care of it but I yelled "no, check on Gary, he may be seriously injured or dead." And you were gone in a flash. To this day I do not know where you came from or how you got to us as fast as you did but I thought then as I do now that God or an angel put you there in a flash. I also remember saying after it was all over "where is my purple heart?" and we all laughed. Doc you did more for your platoon than most who carried guns and fought, and if it were up to most of the guys and I you would have received the Congressional Medal of Honor because you deserved it. So, I said it. I probably won't get serious enough to say it again because between you and I "I have been sitting here half in tears remembering what you did for me and the rest of the platoon. You were and are probably still one of a kind Doc and we all love you for who you are and what you did. You are a brother to us just like everyone else, you did you job a lot better than most and we will never forget it. So in closing you better print and frame this because I won't be this serious again for a while, and maybe you understand why. Anyway take care there brother, make sure you are in Buffalo, and it will be PARTY TIME IN AUG. And remember, TOGETHER THEN, TOGETHER AGAIN.

Wayne Sanders was a good ole' boy from Arkansas who didn't stay
at home long after his previous tour. He quickly came back to the Cav.
He was killed in action in the battle of September 6, 1969.

CHAPTER 13

Ron Halvorsen wrote a book that I really enjoyed called *Prayer Warriors*. The Bible describes Satan as a roaring lion seeking whom he may devour. Again, the Bible talks about putting on the armor of God. Indeed, I fear the sneaky side of the devil more because he attacks and hides in my weaknesses instead of the obvious attacks in the open. Nevertheless, being prepared for the open, powerful attacks will also prepare one to be hanging on to the Lord throughout one's life. God gave me the opportunity of many adventures. I've lived in other countries when young, learned cultures, languages, and acceptance. I've also been forced to make hard decisions in terrible times. I've failed. But I've also been shown the personal love of my Savior, who has never left me despite my multiple failures in the past.

I was raised in a Christian home and was exposed to the knowledge that God was with me. I was raised to be passive. All violence was forbidden. We couldn't even have a squirt gun. I was made meek, if not always as humble as I should be. It made me a target of the strong. I was bullied and laughed at. I was ignored or abused by the powerful and the beautiful. It also made me hang on to the Lord when I couldn't see the next moment. Hard choices were forced on me, but when I was looking for help, he was always there. This book isn't about heroes. I'm not a hero. I just did my job. I never expected or tried for any medals.

The recent movie and books about Desmond Doss demonstrate clearly the need for choice making or, as I call it, having absolutes. Because of Desmond Doss, our lives were easier. While interrogated and verbally abused, I never was placed in a position of physical harm. He made it possible. By the time I got into training, the military had adapted and had special training and duties for us. But the choice making was the same. Let's look at the lifestyle, as an example of all choice making.

The first evening we were in the military was a Friday night. We wanted to go to church. We chose, as a group, to go and talk to the sergeant. We had tons of predicted fears, but we chose to go forward. We found that the sergeant's grandmother was an Adventist. The army didn't need us on that weekend, and he gave us a pass for the Sabbath. I got on the phone while looking through the phone book and dialed the number of the first SDA church in the book. The man who answered happened to be a Middle Eastern man I had known a little at my college. He came and picked all four of us up in his Cadillac. He took us to his church, a black church (as if we cared). There was a good service. There was worship. He took us home to his house for dinner. He then took us back to the post. God was with us every step of that Sabbath. At basic, we had a lot of support from the other recruits and even the sergeants. They not only accepted us, they helped us. We couldn't leave the post, but they made it possible for us to go to the post chapel on the Sabbath until we could go to a church proper. At AIT, we survived the acts of our less religious. God gave me the chance to get extra training. He held up my promotion so that I would go to Vietnam—for his reasons. I grew in experience, knowledge, adjustment, and understanding, which changed my whole life. He showed his protection. There was no good reason at all that I was not seriously hurt or killed except for his intervention. I witnessed before God, often without intent or control. I didn't do all that I should, but neither did I run away. Simply what I was was enough to present another view of looking at God.

Now, let's go back to every step. Understand that every step was a step up on the previous step. Sure, I failed. But I was helped up. The potential discouragement would have been massive if I hadn't gotten up. He gave me the strength. While I carried the fear of death every day, and more so after each fight, I also drew closer to him because he was my only strength.

In World War II, there was the infamous Death March where they took the newly captured, wounded, starving, weak American GIs and marched them a long way without care, food, or water to an eventual railhead for shipping to a camp. Most of those who marched never came home. But the story was that a GI collapsed. The Japanese soldier bayoneted him, pulled him off the trail, got a shovel, and pulled another GI out of the line. He was supposed to dig a grave, put the still living GI in the grave, and then kill him with the shovel. The GI refused. At this point, the Japanese soldier bayoneted the second GI. He then pulled the next GI out and handed him the shovel. What would you do? Praise the Lord I was never put in that position. I can tell you that any such types of decisions are made *now*. There was no time to think about choices. There was no time to prepare. The devil will make it a massively hard, immediate choice. This decision-making is based on an *absolute* part of your soul. I will *not* steal. I will *love*. I will worship. There are no maybes or perhaps. The only way to make that decision is to know it, study it, plan it, live it, now. All of those times someone demanded, "What are you going to do?" helped make it a non-decision. I may not have known how to do certain things, but I knew what I would *not* do. As Joshua said, "Choose ye this day whom ye will serve. But as for me and my house, we will choose the Lord."

Few of us have true absolutes, either positives or negatives. You may have to make terrible choices that never meet your heart or soul. Every Sabbath, are we "worshipping" God? Do we love someone? One of my favorite texts is when Elijah, after having just worshipped the Lord and the prophets of Baal were just killed, got afraid. He ran into the wilderness and hid. God hid him in the cleft of the rock. And God passed before him. God wasn't in the storm; he was in the still small voice. In this complex world with so many ways to distract us, so few of us are listening for God's still, small voice.

I included some letters that were sent to me unsolicited. I assure you that at no time did I ever plan anything looking for praise. God made it possible. I didn't plan; I just lived my life. My man was hurt, and I ran down the possibly mine-strewn road because I needed to go. Yes, I knew that the road might be mined, but I couldn't stop. They needed me. Because God wanted me to be there. There was no choice. It was instinct. I never asked for a medal. My men were what counted. And every one of us today need to be looking for God's children who need you to touch them. You may be the only one who can touch their hearts—which simultaneously opens your heart for blessings. Make the *absolute* choice to serve God. He will do everything you need, small or large. He is always there.

Barry

CPSIA information can be obtained
at www.ICGtesting.com
Printed in the USA
JSHW042009040720
6509JS00006B/111